AF238695

Contents

LEGEND

⧖ Length of walk
◆ Opening times/
   departure times
▲ Transport stop
➤ see

Editor:
Dr. Brigitte Hintzen-Bohlen

Layout:
Andreas Ossig
BKB Verlagsgesellschaft mbh

Translation into English:
John Sykes, Cologne

Printing:
Brandt GmbH, Bonn

ISBN 978-3-96722-042-1

All contents and information
have been conscientiously
researched and carefully
checked. Nevertheless it is not
always possible to avoid errors
entirely. We are therefore
pleased to receive corrections
and proposals for additions.

BKB Verlagsgesellschaft mbh
Auerstraße 4
50733 Köln
Telephone 0221/9521460
Fax 0221/5626446
www.bkb-verlag.de
mail@bkb-verlag.de

This book is:

www.blauer-engel.de/uz195
· ressourcenschonend und umweltfreundlich
  hergestellt
· emissionsarm gedruckt
· aus 100 % Altpapier   **RI1**

Dieses Druckerzeugnis ist mit dem Blauen Engel ausgezeichnet.

Welcome to

... the celebrated town on the river
Neckar which delights visitors from
all over the world with its picturesque ruined castle, historic Old
Town and beautiful surroundings.
The ancient bridge and the Print Media Academy, the old university and
the modern campus at Neuenheimer
Feld, the Church of the Holy Spirit
and Skylabs – it is the meeting of
many contrasts that keeps this city
lively and interesting. An eventful
history of more than 800 years has
left its mark on the town. The foundation of the university in 1386 was
the beginning of Heidelberg's rise to
importance beyond the immediate
region. Initially as a stronghold of
humanism, and after the Reforma-
tion as a centre of Calvinism, the
university attracted students and
researchers from far and wide.

Heidelberg ...

For many centuries prince electors resided in Heidelberg. The castle was extended to house a lavish court, and magnificent Renaissance and Baroque architecture adorned the town. After the destruction of the castle in the War of the Palatinate Succession in the late 17th century and the court's move to Mannheim, a new chapter in Heidelberg's history began following the abolition of the state of the Electoral Palatinate in 1803. The Romantic movement discovered the town, seeing the combination of lovely scenery, a picturesque ruined castle and a historic old quarter as the epitome of urban life. Their paintings and poems made the town on the river Neckar known far and wide, and it became a magnet for tourists that still attracts many visitors today. At the same time the reorganisation of the university in 1803 laid the basis for its revival as a famous place of learning – with such success that Heidelberg enjoys worldwide recognition in the 21st century as a centre of science and research.

With its blend of small-town and international atmosphere, student environment and cosmopolitan openness, Heidelberg still fascinates visitors, inspires artists and stimulates researchers. The town also has a high quality of life. Whether you stroll along the Neckar, climb to the top of the Königstuhl, enjoy the lively and diverse cultural life in the evening or go out for entertainment, in Heidelberg you will discover a wealth of attractive options.

About Heidelberg

● "The city in its setting with all its surroundings has, one could say, something of the ideal ...", wrote Johann Wolfgang von Goethe in 1797. In this he anticipated what the ROMANTICS described in the 19th century when they immortal-ised the town in paintings and poems. Today the picturesque ruined castle above the historic Old Town in the green valley of the Neckar is one of the most visited places in Germany.

● Heidelberg's location makes it one of the warmest places in Germany. On the HEILIGENBERG hill the temperature is actually about 1.5 degrees Celsius higher on average than down in the town: owing to its south-facing slope with a steep gradient of up to 45 degrees and the warming effect of down-winds, it has a remark-able micro-climate in which even almond, fig and olive trees thrive, and excellent conditions for growing grapes.

● The prince electors liked to drink wine, and their cellar in the castle holds the largest barrel that was ever filled with wine. The so-called GREAT BARREL has a capacity of approxi-mately 220,000 litres and was made from the wood of about 90 oak trees from the forests of the Palatinate.

● One of Germany's oldest FUNICULAR RAILWAYS, opened in 1890, takes visitors up to the ruined castle. Its length of 1,020 metres from Kornmarkt up to the Königstuhl makes it one of the longest such railways in Germany.

● In Heidelberg there is also a "HEAVENLY LADDER" of some 1,600 steps that leads from Kornmarkt to the summit of the Königstuhl.

● Founded in 1386, Heidelberg UNIVERSITY is the oldest in Germany and, after the universities in Prague and Vienna, was the third-oldest in the Holy Roman Empire.

● Heidelberg's fame as a CENTRE OF SCIENCE dates back to the 19th century. Here Robert Bunsen and Gustav Robert Kirchhoff invented spectral analysis, Bunsen perfected his Bunsen burner and Hermann von Helmholtz discovered the fundamentals of hydrodynamics.

● Eleven NOBEL PRIZE-WINNERS were researchers at Heidelberg University: Philipp Lenard (Physics, 1905), Albrecht Kossel (Medicine, 1910), Otto Fritz Meyerhof (Medicine, 1922), Richard Kuhn (Chemistry, 1938), Walter Bothe (Physics, 1954), Hans Daniel Jensen (Physics, 1963), Karl Ziegler (Chemistry, 1963), Georg Wittig (Chemistry, 1979), Bert Sakmann (Medicine, 1991), Harald zur Hausen (Medicine, 2008) and Stefan Hell (Chemistry, 2014).

● Heidelberg has not only brought forth famous scientists: in 1943 Silvia Renate Sommerlath, who has been QUEEN OF SWEDEN since 1976, was born here.

● The most popular woman from Heidelberg is probably LISELOTTE, PRINCESS PALATINE, duchess of Orléans and sister-in-law to the "Sun King" Louis XIV. She wrote many thousands of letters describing court life in graphic terms. 5,000 of them have survived.

● Sunshine from Heidelberg: CAPRI-SUN! This fruit drink, more than 50 years old and world market leader in the segment for fruit drinks of up to 0.5 litres, is Germany's best-known juice carton, made of shining plastic and aluminium. CAPRI-SUN is produced in the little town of Eppelheim near Heidelberg.

1. Kornmarkt
2. Karlsplatz
3. Town Hall
4. Marktplatz
5. Hotel zum Ritter
6. Heiliggeistkirche
7. Alte Brücke
8. Friedrich-Ebert-Gedenkstätte
9. Jesuitenkirche
10. Old University / University Museum
11. Student Prison
12. University Library
13. Peterskirche
14. Marstallhof (Mensa)

🍴1 Café Knösel
🍴2 Marstall (Mensa)

Wehrsteg
Karlstor
Schloss-garten
Schloss
Schloßstraße
Jacobsgasse
Friesenberg
Kisselg.
Neckarmünzg.
Haupstraße
Leyerg.
Heiliggeiststraße
Obere Neckar...
Kanzleigasse
Schloßberg
Kurzer Buckel
Schloßberg
Bergbahn
Burgw.
Neue Schloßstraße
Station Kornmarkt
2 Karlsplatz
Am Hackteufel
NECKAR
Ziegelhäuser Landstraße
Mönchgasse
...straße
Fischerg.
3 Rathaus
1 Kornmarkt
Oberbadg.
Mittelbadg.
Apothekerg.
Zwinger Straße
Unterer Fauler Pelz
Neue Schloßstraße
Oberer Fauler Pelz
Schloßberg
7 K.-Theodor-Brücke (Alte Brücke)
4 Marktplatz
6
5 Krämergasse
Pallas Athene
Nauenheimer Landstraße
Haspel-gasse
Pfaffeng.
Floring
Ketten-gasse
Merianstraße
...gasse
Seminarstraße
8 Dreikönig...str.
9 Jesuiten-kirche
Schulgasse
Bussemerg.
Heug.
Augustinergasse
Kleine Mantelg.
Heu-markt
Am Brückentor
Neckarstaden
Lauerstraße
...straße
Mantelgasse
11 10 Alte Universität
Neue Universität
13 Peters-kirche
Grabengasse
12 Universitäts-bibliothek
Marstallstraße
14 Marstall-hof
Sandgasse
Philosophen-gärtchen
Schiffgasse
Theaterstraße
Krahnen-platz
Plöck
ALTSTADT
Friedrich-Ebert-Anlage
Untere
Haupstraße
Friedrichstraße
Bauamtsgasse
Neckarstaden...straße
Providenz-kirche
K.-Ludwig-Str.
Bienenstraße
Landfriedstraße
Kongresshaus Stadthalle
Karpfengasse
März-garten

N
250 m

City Walk

CHARLES DE GRAIMBERG (1774-1864)

When this French aristocrat came to the Neckar valley in 1810 to do some sketching, the castle ruin captivated him so much that he settled in Heidelberg and made its preservation his life's work. At that time it was being used only as a source of cheap stone. Graimberg rented rooms in the castle in the gatehouse tower of the Gläserner Saalbau, made and sold engravings of his Romantic views of the castle, and spent part of his fortune in restoring the buildings. Graimberg thus became the first restorer and the saviour of Heidelberg Castle! In his house on Kornmarkt he assembled a cabinet of curiosities with items that he found in the castle and the town. After his death this collection became the basis for the Kurpfälzisches Museum.

THE PEARL ON THE NECKAR – A CITY WALK

This walk through the Old Town takes you past historic buildings, along crooked alleyways and to little squares, where you will agree with Scheffel, who wrote enthusiastically: "Old Heidelberg, thou city fine, rich in honours on Neckar and Rhine, none compares with thee."

● KORNMARKT: This walk through the Old Town begins on the idyllic little square that was laid out in the 16th century on the site of the old hospital as a marketplace for milk and vegetables. It is surrounded by historic buildings such as the Palais Graimberg at the south-east corner and the *Palais Prinz Carl* on its west side. The much-visited attraction at its centre is the Kornmarkt Madonna, a Baroque statue of the Virgin Mary on a globe that is borne by putti (the original is in the Kurpfälzisches Museum). It was erected on a column in 1718 during the Counter-Reformation and was placed on the fountain at the centre of the square in 1830.

● KARLSPLATZ: From this broad square, which takes its name from Grand Duke Karl Friedrich of Baden, there is a fine view of the castle. At the centre a modern fountain commemorates the humanist and

cosmographer Sebastian Münster, who began his famous work *Cosmographia* from 1521 to 1529 in the Franciscan monastery which once stood here. To the south the square is bounded by the Baroque *Grand Ducal Palace*, now the seat of the Heidelberg Academy of Sciences. The *Palais Boisserée* opposite, in which the Boisserée brothers once exhibited their art collection, now held by the Alte Pinakothek in Munich, is home to the Germanisches Institut. A few paces further on you reach the well-known historic student pubs *Zum Seppl* (1704) and *Zum Roten Ochsen* (1724), where generations of student fraternities have held their celebrations.

● MARKTPLATZ:

The market-
place is
the main
square
of the
Old Town.
When the
sun shines there
is a Mediterranean
atmosphere here. The numerous pubs and cafés put out their tables and chairs, inviting passers-by to stop for a while. This is a wonderful spot for admiring the historic buildings round about. The Baroque Rathaus (town hall) stands on the east side, the coat of arms of the prince electors above its large balcony. Take a look at the adjoining building with a turret and glockenspiel, which plays songs such as *Old Heidelberg*. At the corner of Apothekergasse stands a conspicuous Baroque building with the colourful coat of arms of the prince electors. This was once the court apothecary's shop, which had the exclusive right to supply medicine to the prince elector's court.

MEMBERS, FOXES AND OLD GENTLEMEN

In historic student drinking dens, yellowing photos, lithographs, drinking horns and other trophies serve as reminders of the merry life of student corps. These fraternities were founded in the 19th century by students who were engaged in the struggle for national unification of Germany, and today membership is regarded as an admission ticket to a position in society and business. Those "foxes" who successfully pass through the probation period to become members remain in the association all their lives. The support that they receive from the fraternity during their time as a student is then repaid once they have entered professional life and attain the status of *Alter Herr* (Old Gentleman – or Old Lady). To this day there are more than 30 fraternities in Heidelberg with over 800 students, who on official occasions usually wear colours, consisting of a student cap known as a *Couleur* and a ribbon in the colours of the corps. In the more traditional fraternities the practice of academic fencing with sharp blades, called *Mensur*, is still part of the communal life.

KARLSTOR

The eastern end of the main street, Hauptstraße, is marked by a triumphal arch that the citizens of Heidelberg erected to honour Prince Elector Karl Theodor. This classical work in the Roman tradition, built between 1775 and

1781 to plans by Nicolas de Pigage, is crowned by four Palatinate lions. On the city side, portraits of the elector and his wife decorate the Karlstor, and on its outer façade arriving visitors can read a dedicatory inscription beneath the coat of arms of the Electoral Palatinate, flanked by two lions.

● HOTEL ZUM RITTER: One of the finest buildings is the inn opposite the Heiliggeistkirche, the only one – according to the inscription on the gable, "Persta invicta, Venus" (Remain always undefeated, o beauty) – to have survived all the wars and fires in Heidelberg. Built in 1592 by the wealthy Huguenot cloth dealer Charles Bélier as a six-storey residence, for over 300 years it has been an inn. The Ritter (knight) who gave the building its name is Saint George, who can be seen up on the gable. The impressive Renaissance façade of ashlar masonry is adorned with fluted columns, beautifully carved window frames and a wealth of ornamentation.

Hauptstraße 178, www.zum-ritter-heidelberg.de/en

● HEILIGGEISTKIRCHE: The Church of the Holy Spirit, a Gothic hall church with a Baroque roof and tower-top, dominates the Marktplatz. Constructed in 1398 as a burial church for the prince electors of the Palatinate, it has had an eventful history. Sometimes Catholic, sometimes Protestant, after the War of the Palatinate Succession it was even a place of worship for both confessions, who held their services in the choir and nave of the church, divided by a wall. This situation, commemorated by a plaque in the right-hand aisle on the steps to the choir, explains why there are exits on both sides. Since 1936 the church has been used by the Lutheran congregation.

The proportions of the interior, with its extremely wide aisles, are unusual. The reason is that the galleries were used in the Middle

Ages as a lecture hall for the university and also housed, among other things, a famous library, the Biblioteca Palatina. The only item among the once-magnificent furnishings and the tombs of the prince electors to have survived iconoclasm and destruction is the grave slab of Elector Ruprecht III, builder of the castle, and his wife Elisabeth von Hohenzollern, which bears royal insignia. In the nave note the 15th-century ceiling painting of a concert of angels – though the bassoon was added by a restorer in the 1950s!

In good weather do not fail to climb the 200 steps to the top of the tower, for which a wonderful view of the ruined castle and the Neckar valley is the reward.

The stalls around the nave of the church are a relic of the Middle Ages. Originally religious articles such as rosaries and saints' images were sold in these booths, but later bread and meat were sold there, and craftsmen set up shop too. A reminiscence of this are the pretzels carved in the sandstone, which served for making comparisons with the size of those that were actually sold.

▶ www.ekihd.de

BIBLIOTHECA PALATINA

The Lorsch Gospels, the Codex Manesse, the Falconry Book of Emperor Frederick II and the Ottheinrich Bible are just a few of the treasures that once belonged to the Bibliotheca Palatina. The "mother of all libraries" was created in the reign of the book-loving Elector Ottheinrich (reigned 1556-59) by amalgamating the collections of the university, the collegiate library of the Heiliggeistkirche and the library of the elector's palace. However, as the university was Protestant, the library was regarded by Catholics as a hotbed of heresy, and after the conquest of Heidelberg by the forces of the Catholic League in 1622 the holdings of 3,500 manuscripts and 12,000 books and prints were taken to Rome as a gift to the papacy. Some manuscripts were

returned to Heidelberg after the Congress of Vienna, but most of them remain to this day in the Biblioteca Apostolica Vaticana.

TIP Treat your soul to a short break and relax to the music that is played in the lunch-time service of the Heiliggeistkirche on Thu-Sat (Eastern-Oct.).

THE BRIDGE MONKEY

There is always a crowd of people around the modern figure of a monkey next to the bridge tower. It is a great motif for photos, and it is possible to put your head inside that of the monkey. The figure is also said to possess magic powers: if you stroke the extended finger on its right paw, you will certainly return to Heidelberg, and if you stroke its rear, you will

be prosperous. The historic function of the monkey was different. Originally placed on the bridge tower on the opposite side of the town, it displayed its naked backside to people who arrived and thus demonstrated that the authority of the bishops of Mainz ended at that point.

● ALTE BRÜCKE (KARL-THEODOR-BRÜCKE): Walk along Steingasse to the Old Bridge, which was described in enthusiastic terms by Goethe, Hölderlin and many others, and is a favourite place to meet to this day. It is named after Elector Karl Theodor, who built a stone bridge consisting of barrel vaults of red sandstone in 1786–88 to replace its wooden predecessor. The fact that the bridge was once fortified is shown on the town side by the surviving gateway flanked by twin towers, where the warden of the bridge once lived.

To express their thanks for this first stone bridge, the people of Heidelberg erected a monument to their ruler, showing the prince elector surrounded by the gods of the main rivers of the Palatinate. On the Neuenheim side of the bridge a statue of Pallas Athene, with four allegorical figures at her feet symbolising justice, piety, agriculture and trade, is a reference to the elector's government of his land, as are the representations of the arts and sciences in the reliefs of the base with cherubs. The statue of Saint John Nepomuk was taken from the previous bridge. In the Palatinate, which had just become a Catholic state, this was a deliberate symbol of the Counter-Reformation. When the statue fell into the river during the floods of 1784 it was not returned to the bridge but placed close to it on the river bank.

● REICHSPRÄSIDENT-FRIEDRICH-EBERT-GEDENKSTIFTUNG: Now walk past the little houses of the Old Town through Haspelgasse and Untere Straße to the birthplace of the first democratically elected German head of state, Friedrich Ebert (1871–1925). Here you can get a good impression of the living conditions of a family of artisans in the late 19th century. Eight persons lived without electricity and running water on an area of 46 square metres, which served during the day as a workshop for the father, a tailor.

A permanent exhibition, which is also housed in the adjoining buildings, gives information about the life and times of Friedrich Ebert. Many original documents, photos and other items reflect the history of the workers' movement and German political history between the imperial period and the Weimar Republic.

Pfaffengasse 18
www.ebert-gedenkstaette.de

FRIEDRICH EBERT (1871-1925)

He is one of many famous people who were laid to rest in the Bergfriedhof cemetery (➤ p. 59). Born in Heidelberg in 1871, the seventh of nine children of the tailor Karl Ebert, he was apprenticed to a saddler after leaving school. An active trade unionist, he moved with his family to Bremen, where he was elected to the city parliament and became workers' secretary of the labor union. After

election to the central committee of the SPD he moved to Berlin in 1905, was a member of the Reichstag from 1912 and one of the three chairmen of the SPD parliamentary party there from 1916. After the November Revolution Ebert became president of the Weimar Republic on 11 February 1919. As the first democratically elected head of state, he was a pioneer of German parliamentary democracy.

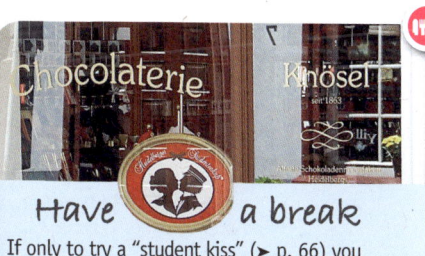

Have a break

If only to try a "student kiss" (➤ p. 66) you should definitely make a stop at the old-established **Café Knösel**. *Haspelgasse 20* *www.cafeknoesel-hd.de*

HEIDELBER-GER HERBST

On the last Saturday in September the Old Town (Altstadt) of Heidelberg is transformed into one big festival, at which craft workers set up their stalls along the Hauptstraße, a flea market spreads through the little alley-ways, and the stands on the banks of the Neckar tempt people to stroll by and taste regional speciali-ties. All of this is comple-mented by a big programme of music and theatre that is held from midday on large and small stages on the various squares of the town. The festival also

caters to younger visitors with a children's flea mar-ket and special programme for families.

www.heidelberg-marketing.de

● JESUITENKIRCHE: The Catholic counterpart to the Church of the Holy Spirit is the aisled hall church in the former Jesuit quarter of the Old Town. Construction started in the early 18th century and lasted about 150 years. It was intended that the Jesuits, who came to Heidelberg in 1622 during the Thirty Years' War and worked in the university or as school teachers and in parochial care, would promote the Counter-Reformation by supporting the Catholic prince electors. Thus the richly decorated main façade of the church with its statues of Ignatius Loyola, the founder of the Jesuit order, on the left, and of Saint Francis Xavier on the right, was modelled on the Jesuit mother church, Il Gesu in Rome. Nothing remains of the Baroque fittings inside, but the entirely white interior with gilded capitals and altars adorned with frescoes is an attractive sight.

To find out more about the work of the Jesuits in the Electoral Palatinate, visit the *Museum für sakrale Kunst und Liturgie* (Museum of Religious Art and Liturgy) in the church, which also dis-plays saints' images, chalices and monstrances, priests' robes and a large silver Madonna by J. Ignaz Saller dating from 1736.

Merianstraße 2
www.stadtkirche-heidelberg.de

3 TIP To take some time out, go through the left-hand side entrance to the *Meditation Garden* of the Jesuit Church. Here, away from the bustle of the pedestrian zone, you can watch bees col-lecting nectar or simply admire the numer-ous plants and flowers.

The University

THE UNIVERSITY STORY

When Count Palatinate and Prince Elector Ruprecht I founded Heidelberg University in 1386 with the permission of Pope Urban VI, it was the third university in the Holy Roman Empire and the first in what is today Germany, and had four faculties: theology, law, medicine and philosophy.

The university had its first age of greatness in the second half of the 16th century, when Elector Ottheinrich made it into a Protestant place of learning for his state. It became a European centre of science and culture, gaining a reputation as a stronghold of Calvinism, to which the Heidelberg Catechism in Protestant churches is testimony to this day.

SEMPER APERTUS – THE UNIVERSITY

In Germany's oldest university you can immerse yourself in the world of science and research, get to know places of learning, see old prison cells and the new dining hall, and begin to understand how a living tradition arose in the course of centuries.

● **ALTE UNIVERSITÄT:** The tour of various university sites begins at Universitätsplatz in the middle of the pedestrian zone. The square where students now gather around a fountain with the lion of the Palatinate was once the site of the Augustinian monastery, the largest and wealthiest in the town, where the first lectures were held and Martin Luther presented his theses in 1518. After French forces destroyed the old university complex in 1693, a new main building was constructed on the north side of the square, known as the Alte Universität (Old University). Its motto "Semper

apertus" (meaning that the book of knowledge should always be open) is to be seen in big letters in the foyer.

● **UNIVERSITÄTSMUSEUM:** The three rooms of the university museum on the ground floor offer a good overview of the 600-year history of the university. Exhibits, portraits and documents bear witness to the spirit of past times, and special exhibitions present a wider view of the activities of the university.

● AULA: Don't miss the room in which lectures and disputations were held. Newly fitted out in 1886 for the 500th anniversary of the university in Italian Renaissance style with magnificent wood panelling and paintings, the Aula is an impressive original location of university life. The end wall was designed as a triumphal arch with a bust of Grand Duke Friedrich of Baden, ruler of the Palatinate at that time and also rector of the university, at its centre. On either side of it two portraits can be seen: on the left Prince Elector Ruprecht I, founder of the university, on the right Margrave Karl Friedrich of Baden, who reorganised the university in 1803. Above it Pallas Athene enters Heidelberg with her retinue – rectors, researchers and the bishop of Worms, all of them persons who were active at the university over the centuries – to symbolise the entrance of wisdom with the foundation of the university. On the ceiling representations of the four original faculties – theology, jurisprudence, medicine and philosophy – can be admired. The name plates on the seats are a reference to the great numbers of renowned researchers and professors who worked here.

Grabengasse 1
www.uni-heidelberg.de

THE UNIVERSITY STORY

Following reorganisation in 1803 by the first Grand Duke of Baden, Karl Friedrich, after which the university was named Ruperto Carola, a second period of renown began. Heidelberg was widely seen as a university for lawyers, and the collaboration of Robert Bunsen, Hermann Helmholtz, Gustav Kirchhoff and Max Weber led to a golden age in the natural sciences, which became the fifth faculty in 1891. The third great period began in the 21st century. With more than 30,000 students, the Ruperto Carola University at its three sites in the Old Town (humanities and social sciences), Bergheim (sociology, political and economic sciences) and Neuenheimer Feld (natural sciences, medicine) has an excellent reputation for research, was successful in the German "Excellence Initiative" for universities and occupies a leading position in internationally acknowledged rankings.

● **STUDENT PRISON:** For another sight that makes a strong impression, go to the rear side of the Alte Universität to see the cells (Karzer) in which students were imprisoned between 1778 and 1914. As the university exercised its own judicial rights at that time, it could place students under arrest for up to four weeks for minor offences such as fencing too violently, disturbing the peace at night and unruly behaviour. While serving the sentence, the students were obliged to attend lectures, but spent the rest of the time in the Karzer. This was a severe punishment in the early decades, as the prisoners were given only bread and water and slept on straw on the cold floor. From about 1900 the rules were relaxed and visitors permitted. The students then used the Karzer as a meeting place for making merry and playing cards. It gradually became fashionable for them to spend a few days in the prison at least once during their time as a student. The fates of those who were incarcerated here can be seen in thousands of graffiti that cover all the walls.

Augustinergasse 2
www.uni-heidelberg.de

● **CITY OF SCIENCE:** Heidelberg has a top position for science, as its university is not only the oldest in Germany but also one of the best. This is demonstrated by the high number of patent registrations and eleven Nobel Prizes that have been awarded to professors at Heidelberg University. Several other institutions of higher education are based here, among them a school of Jewish Studies, a school of church music, a teachers' college, the SRH Hochschule and the Schiller International University. Renowned

science and research institutes such as the German Cancer Research Center, the European Laboratory for Molecular Biology, four Max Planck Institutes, the Academy of Sciences and Humanities and the Heidelberg Institute for Theoretical Studies are based in Heidelberg.

● UNIVERSITY LIBRARY: Walk past the Neue Universität, built in 1930–31 integrating the Witches' Tower of the medieval city wall, to reach what must be the university's finest building. Constructed with four wings in 1905 with numerous oriels, turrets, gables and sculptures, the Universitätsbibliothek (University Library) combines elements of German Mannerism of the late 16th century with Art Nouveau motifs. Two figures on the main entrance – on the left Prometheus, on the right a female figure with a child symbolising the passing on of knowledge from generation to generation – frame the way to the interior, where busts of famous scholars can be seen in the staircase. Glance inside the lovely green courtyard, an idyllic spot for a rest. The university library, which has over 3 million books and 1.5 million loans each year, is one of Germany's leading libraries, and the building is always a busy place. The special attraction for visitors, in addition to many medieval treasures, donations and bequests by prince electors and professors, and interesting exhibitions, is the Codex Manesse, a world-famous medieval book of songs on 426 leaves of parchment, inscribed on both sides. It is kept in the reading room for manuscripts, the *Handschriftenlesesaal*.

Plöck 107–109
www.ub.uni-heidelberg.de

GERMAN CANCER RESEARCH CENTER

With more than 3,000 employees, the *German Cancer Research Center (Deutsches Krebsfor-schungszentrum, DKFZ)* is Germany's largest biomedical research institute. DKFZ scientists identify cancer risk factors, investigate how cancer progresses and develop new cancer prevention strategies. They are also developing new methods to diagnose tumors more precisely and treat cancer patients more successfully. The importance of this research is demonstrated by two Nobel Prizes awarded to DKFZ scientists (2008: Harald zur Hausen, 2014: Stefan Hell). To transfer promising approaches from cancer research to the clinic and thus improve the prognosis of cancer patients, the DKFZ cooperates with excellent research institutions and university hospitals throughout Germany. The DKFZ's Cancer Information Service provides patients, their relatives and experts with individual answers to questions relating to cancer.

www.dkfz.de

ARCHAEOLOGICAL TEACHING COLLECTION

The plaster casts of ancient sculptures in the Marstallhof can be seen through the panes of glass. Via the Horse Tamers of Monte Cavallo you go to the *Abguss-Sammlung* (Cast Collection), which provides an illuminating survey

of the development of Greek sculpture from its beginnings until the Roman imperial period – not only for students. To view originals, go to the *Antikenmuseum* on the top floor, where painted ceramics, terracotta works, coins and bronze jewellery from ancient Mediterranean civilisations are on display.

Neues Kollegiengebäude, Marstallhof 4
◆ *currently closed*
www.uni-heidelberg.de/ fakultaeten/philosophie/ zaw/klarch/index.html

● **PETERSKIRCHE:** Opposite the library is St Peter's Church, the oldest in the town, a place of burial for scholars. In the late 19th century it was rebuilt in Gothic Revival style as a hall church with aisles and adorned with monumental paintings such as two pictures of Christ by Hans Thoma and the Sermon on the Mount by Fritz Mackensen on the north gallery. Today its artistic treasures include nine modern stained-glass windows by Johannes Schreiter.

Plöck 70
www.peterskirche-heidelberg.de

● **MARSTALL:** To conclude the tour we go towards the banks of the Neckar to the so-called Marstall, which served as an arsenal for the castle and was defended by corner towers because it was situated outside the town walls. The name of the building refers to the use of the now-destroyed south wing for stables, with accommodation on the upper floor above them. Today this late medieval complex, which has been altered many times, houses the student dining hall, the Mensa. It is worth taking a look at the rubblestone building with a Baroque semi-hipped roof. This was the municipal tithe barn, in which hay for the horses of the Marstall was stored until 1824. It is now used for lectures.

Have a break

Visitors too find the students' Mensa a pleasant spot, either in the green courtyard or in the **Marstall** building itself!
Marstallhof 3

Heidelberg by Night

TECHNOLOGIEPARK

The concentration of institutions of higher education, science and research in Heidelberg makes the town a sought-after location for companies associated with research. The Technologiepark effectively supports the innovations that arise from the co-operation of companies with educational and research institutions. It is no coincidence that Heidelberg is now one of the leading places for biotechnology both in Germany and worldwide. Since it was founded in 1984 at Neuenheimer Feld, the Technologiepark has had to be enlarged constantly. Its six sites now make an area of 100,000 square metres available. Thanks to its mix of biotechnology, medical technology, organic electronics, and information and communication technology, it has become a major provider of impulses for science and the economy.

www.technologiepark-heidelberg.de/en
www.dkfz.de

OUT ON THE TOWN – HEIDELBERG BY NIGHT

Heidelberg's nightlife has a lot to offer. Whether you want culture or dancing, a student pub or a cool bar, this university town has the right locations for everyone.

Plenty of alternatives are available if you plan to enjoy a cultural evening. With its five departments – opera, concerts, drama, dance and youth theatre – the *Theater und Orchester Heidelberg* alone offers a wide choice. Small private theatres such as the *Taeter-Theater* and the *Zimmertheater* are also firmly established on the cultural scene. Concerts given by the *Collegium Musicum* and the *Sinfonieorchester TonArt* enrich the musical programme,

THE RIVER NECKAR

In good weather you should not miss a boat trip through the Neckartal-Odenwald Natural Park, either along the Burgenstraße (Castle Road) or downstream to the biggest industrial region on the river Rhine. Today, on its way to the Rhine, the Neckar flows quietly and slowly through Heidelberg, where it has carved out

and jazz fans are catered for down in the vaults of the *Jazzhaus*. For cinema lovers in particular, Heidelberg is a delight, as a number of ambitious art-house cinemas find interested audiences in university circles (➤ p. 60 ff.).

TIP If you want to know what is going on in Heidelberg, take a look at the listings in: *www.stadtleben.de/heidelberg/kalender/* or *www.heidelberg-marketing.de.*

If you would rather go dancing, then head for the Old Town, where you will find the hotspots of Heidelberg's nightlife around the marketplace in the streets *Untere Straße* and *Steingasse*. Here is a concentration of little cocktail bars, pleasant cafés and pubs in a small area, and the atmosphere on warm summer nights is reminiscent of southern Europe. When the first rays of sun appear, tables and chairs are placed outdoors, and the life of the town takes place in the narrow

the deepest part of its valley between hills that are more than 400 metres high. However, it was not always gentle, as the word "Neckar" itself suggests. The name is of Celtic origin and means "wild water". It was not until its conversion to a river navigation in the 1920s that the river was tamed in its course, and the frequent changes in water level and the numerous cliffs no longer presented a problem to shipping.

www.weisseflottehd.de

MADE BY HEIDELBERG

Print Media Academy and (S)printing Horse are just two of many emblems of Heidelberg that show its status as a dynamic place of business: Heidelberg is more than a tourist attraction. Companies that are based here include global leaders such as Heidelberg Materials AG, a major supplier of building materials;

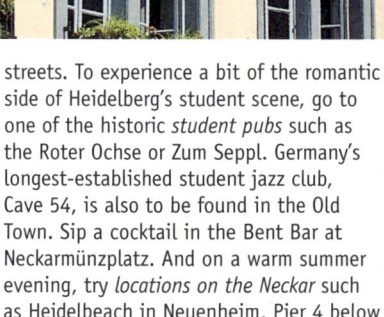

Heidelberger Druckmaschinen AG, known all over the world for its offset printing machines; Technology group ABB Stotz-Kontakt, a supplier of safety automation; big names in the IT industry such as SAP and the SAS Institute; and the ProMinent-Group, an international leader in water technology. Here Lamy produces pens that have won awards all over the world, and WILD makes a popular fruit drink called Capri-Sun. Heidelberg is also home to Springer Nature, a global academic publishing company.

streets. To experience a bit of the romantic side of Heidelberg's student scene, go to one of the historic *student pubs* such as the Roter Ochse or Zum Seppl. Germany's longest-established student jazz club, Cave 54, is also to be found in the Old Town. Sip a cocktail in the Bent Bar at Neckarmünzplatz. And on a warm summer evening, try *locations on the Neckar* such as Heidelbeach in Neuenheim, Pier 4 below the Stadthalle or the Bootshaus, the club pub of the Heidelberg rowing society.

When the pubs close, the *dance clubs* are just getting going. There are lots of places to dance the night away, from small clubs in the Old Town such as Toniq and Halle02 in the Bahnstadt or the Kulturhaus Karlstorbahnhof.

The Castle

ROMANTIC HEIDELBERG

The picturesque castle ruin inspired the Romantics, delighted countless students who came to the university after its reorganisation, and was celebrated by visitors as a place where a glorified view of the past had visibly found its home. For people of the Romantic age, Heidelberg was the incarnation of the ideal town. Clemens Brentano, Achim von Arnim, Joseph von Görres und Joseph von Eichendorff praised the town in song and poetry, and painters such as Karl Philipp Fohr and J.M.W. Turner depicted the ruin in famous pictures. If you would like to find out more about the reception of the castle in the Romantic age, visit the permanent exhibition in the Ruprechtsbau.

TESTIMONY TO A GLORIOUS PAST – THE CASTLE

The ascent of the Königstuhl takes you to one of Europe's best-known ruined castles, the centre of power and prestige of the prince electors for five centuries and, thanks to the enthusiasm of 19th-century Romantics, the emblem of Heidelberg.

When Elector Ruprecht III (reigned 1398–1410) extended an early 13th-century castle to make it his seat of power, he laid the foundation for a splendid palace. Continually enlarged by his successors, over the centuries it became an architectural ensemble with some of the finest Renaissance buildings in Germany. Its history did not end until the War of the Palatinate Succession, when French troops destroyed the castle after capturing the town, and Prince Elector Karl Philipp moved his residence to Mannheim in 1720. If a French aristocrat, Count Charles de Graimberg (➤ p. 10), had not campaigned for the preservation of the castle ruins and made views of them known all over the world through prints, only a few stones would remain today.

The easiest way to go up to the castle is to take the funicular railway. Before starting the castle tour, it is worth making a short detour to the Stückgarten, so called because it was laid out for the cannon (Stücke) of Elector Ludwig V (reigned 1508–44). Because this spot commands a beautiful view of Heidelberg, Elector Friedrich V demolished the greater part of the fortifications here in 1615 and created a pleasure garden with a gate like a triumphal arch, the Elisabethentor, as a gift for his wife Elizabeth Stuart on her 19th birthday.

To reach the castle courtyard you have to cross the Hirschgraben (Stag Ditch), in which stags

THE WITCH'S BITE

Look out for the thick iron knocker, a ring on the little door that has been cut out of the wooden gate at the entrance for security reasons. The small hollow in the iron is said to derive from the bite of a witch! As one of the prince electors had no children to succeed him, according to a legend he promised power to whoever could bite through the thick knocker on the door. If anyone was strong enough to do so, he believed, they would also be strong enough to rule. Many noblemen tried it, but it was a witch who almost succeeded, until at the last moment her teeth fell out.

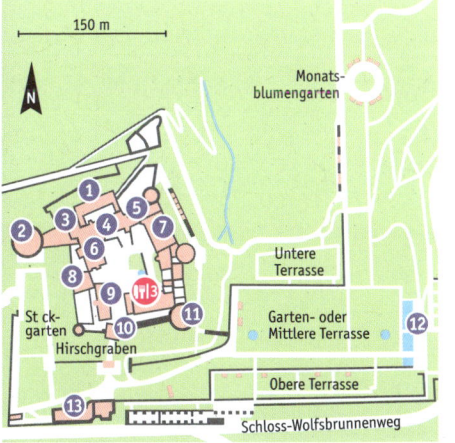

1 Großer Altan
    (castle terrace)
2 Dicker Turm
3 Fassbau
4 Friedrichsbau
5 Gläserner Saalbau
6 Frauenzimmerbau
7 Ottheinrichsbau and
    Apothekermuseum
8 Bibliotheksbau
9 Ruprechtsbau
10 Torturm mit Hexenring
11 Krautturm
12 Fountain with
    Father Rhine
13 Visitor Centre

THE GREAT BARREL

In front of the façade of the Friedrichsbau you descend at an angle on the left to the wine cellar of the electors, home to the Großes Fass, one of the castle's main attractions. This barrel, built for Elector Karl Theodor (reigned 1742-99) by his cellarer Johann Jakob Englert using 90 oak trees from the forests of the Palatinate, holds some 220,000 litres. After being used three times it started to leak and was never filled again.

Like its three predecessors, the barrel, which is seven metres wide and 8.5 metres long, supports a dance floor on which the court could hold merry celebrations. The wine cellar itself dates from the period of the first barrel, when Elector Johann Casimir (reigned 1588–93) ordered construction of a barrel "like no other on earth" with a capacity of almost 128,000 litres.

and bears were kept in the 17th century, passing through the house of the bridge keeper and going over a stone bridge to a rectangular gate tower with a heavy wooden door. The oldest residential building in the castle, the Ruprechtsbau, built for Elector Ruprecht III (reigned 1398–1410), is on the left in the courtyard. A coat of arms with the imperial eagle is a reference to the fact that this prince elector was also king of the Germans, with the title Ruprecht I of the Palatinate. Above the entrance you see two angels with a wreath of five roses. According to tradition this commemorates two sons of a master builder who were killed during construction work. The grieving father became a recluse and brought a fresh wreath of roses to the construction site every day until his sons appeared to him in a dream and consoled him. From that moment he returned to the job and immortalised his children in stone.

Next to it is the late-Gothic Bibliotheksbau (library) with its fine oriel on the upper floor, built in the reign of Elector Ludwig V (1508–1544). The adjacent Frauenzimmerbau, of which only the

Have a break

After your visit, take refreshments offered by the **Heidelberger Schloss Restaurants & Events GmbH** on the terrace in front of the old domestic buildings or in the historic bakery.
www.heidelberger-schloss-gastronomie.de

ground floor remains, probably accommodated ladies of court on its upper floors, while the great royal hall beneath was used for daily meals and festivities. Today it is used as a hall for events.

> **3 TIP** Don't fail to put your foot in the Rittersprung (knight's leap)! This foot-shaped depression in the stone is said to be the print of a young nobleman who was caught in flagrante with the young wife of an elector and made his escape by jumping from a window. It is said that anyone whose foot fits into the hole will have a happy life.

On the north side of the courtyard stands the magnificent Friedrichsbau. The elector who built it, Friedrich IV (reigned 1583–1610), adorned its façade with his ancestors from the House of Wittelsbach – from Charlemagne to Ludwig of Bavaria – in order to legitimise his rule. The castle chapel on the ground floor escaped destruction and is used for weddings today. To the right of the Friedrichsbau a passage leads to the Altan, a terrace with a view of the valley. From here you have a superb panorama of Heidelberg's Old Town, the river Neckar and its valley down towards the plain of the Rhine.

To the right of the entrance you see the Gläserner Saalbau with its massive arches dating from the time of Elector Friedrich II (reigned 1544–56). The building takes its name (Glass Hall) from the Venetian mirrors that embellished

PERKEO

Opposite the Great Barrel is a painted wooden figure of the famous dwarf Perkeo, whom visitors to Heidelberg encounter in many places. Elector Karl Philipp is said to have brought a hard-drinking dwarf named Clemens from Tyrol to his court to be his steward and master of ceremonies. As the court dwarf responded to every offer of a drink with the words "Perche No?" ("Why not?"), he quickly acquired his nickname. His ability to hold his drink was so famous that he was celebrated in many poems. Viktor von Scheffel wrote: "The dwarf Perkeo At Heidelberg's court Is a giant at drinking Though his stature is short."

Perkeo is reported by legend to have died in his eighties because he took the doctor's advice to drink a glass of water instead of wine, and died of dysentery.

![image]()

the hall on the upper floor. A few years later Elector Ottheinrich (reigned 1556-59) constructed the Ottheinrichsbau on the east side. Its elaborate courtly façade is regarded as one of the finest examples of Renaissance architecture in Germany. Framed by two staircase towers and adorned with a portal in the form of a triumphal arch, it is impressive above all for the rich sculptural work on the façade showing figures from the Bible and ancient times to symbolise the rule of the prince elector. This and the adjoining building are now home to a museum of pharmacy, the Deutsches Apotheken-Museum.

www.deutsches-apotheken-museum.de

Before leaving the castle it is worth taking a walk past the Krautturm, a tower with masonry that was blown up by the French, through the large palace garden, the Hortus Palatinus, which occupies five terraces high above the Neckar. When the garden was created (1615–19) it was regarded as one of the leading examples of Renaissance horticulture, an eighth wonder of the world. Today only a few details such as the big grotto with Father Rhine testify to past glories. Finish your visit by standing on the Scheffelterrasse in the north-east of the garden to enjoy the view of the castle ruins and the valley of the Neckar.

Schlosshof 1 (Königstuhl)
▲ *Bergbahn*
www.schloss-heidelberg.de

KÖNIGSTUHL: Fit walkers take the Himmelsleiter (heavenly ladder) from Kornmarkt, a picturesque stairway built in 1844 with about 1,600 steps, but most people take the Bergbahn (funicular railway) via the stations Schloss and Molkenkur to the top of the Königstuhl.

At 567.8 metres it is the highest point in the Kleiner Odenwald, with a wonderful view of the Neckar valley, the plain of the Rhine and in good weather as far as Alsace. Here you can walk on various trails, take children to discover Snow White and other fairytale figures in the *Märchenparadies* and watch birds of prey in the *Falknerei Tinnunculus*.

www.maerchen-paradies.de
www.tinnunculus-heidelberg.de

Philosophers' Path

THE HEILIGENBERG

As early as 450 BC the 440-metre Heiligenberg (Holy Mount) was a place of settlement. Around the summit Celts built an encircling wall five kilometres long as a defence against the advance of Germanic peoples. This is now one of the largest extant Celtic fortifications and is still visible on the ground. The Heidenloch (Heathen Hole), a 50-metre-deep shaft that is shrouded in myth, was probably used for religious purposes. In the Nazi period the hill was deprived of its Celtic connection and hailed as a "Germanic cult site". In 1934 the Thingstätte (a "Thing" was an ancient Germanic place of assembly) was constructed here with 8,000 seats and standing room for a further 5,000 persons. It has survived, as has the early Romanesque ruin of St Michael's and St Stephen's monastery.

IN THE FOOTSTEPS OF POETS AND THINKERS – THE PHILOSOPHERS' PATH

The walk called Philosophenweg crosses the Neckar and follows one of Germany's most beautiful paths, commanding a magnificent panoramic view of the castle and the Old Town of Heidelberg.

It makes no real difference where you begin the three-kilometre walk, as you have to climb 120 metres whichever option you decide to take, but the gentle ascent, most suitable for people who are not experienced walkers, starts in the Neuenheim district of the town. From Ladenburger Straße the path climbs in steep curves to a point halfway up the Heiligenberg, passing the Physikalisches Institut of the university and some fine detached houses with gardens full of trees, which you can stop to admire. When you have reached house

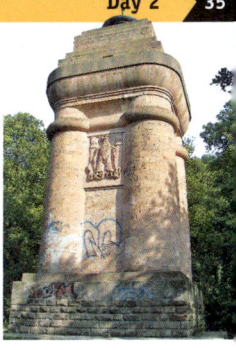

no. 21 you can breathe a sigh of relief, as the climb is over and you are rewarded with a first lovely view of the Kongresshalle and restaurant ship.

In 1841, when this path through the vineyards was widened, no-one could have imagined that it would become one of Germany's most famous walks. It gained its name in the Romantic period, when young philosophers, as students were then called because they had to study philosophy for several terms before the beginning of their specialised courses, used to meet here for a romantic stroll or an undisturbed tête-à-tête. Poets and thinkers such as Hölderlin, Eichendorff, Scheffel and many others came here to relax, and walked through the vineyards to give free rein to their thoughts.

The first stop, where the Bismarcksäulenweg branches off, is a reminder of this era: the *Philosophengärtchen*, a little garden with flower beds where stands a bust of the Romantic poet

BISMARCK COLUMN

There is another fine view from the lookout platform of the Bismarcksäule. The upper path that branches off at the Philosophengärtchen leads there. The Bismarck Column in Heidelberg dates from 1903, when such towers were erected all over Germany to honour the founder of the Reich, Otto von Bismarck. The architect Wilhelm Kreis produced a standard design for them named "twilight of the gods", and this version was used in Heidelberg. The 15-metre-high square tower of red sandstone with three-quarter columns at the corners is adorned on the side facing the town by a relief of the imperial eagle with the snake of discord. At the top of the tower is a cast-iron cauldron with a diameter of 2.5 metres, used by student fraternities to light a fire on certain days of the year such as Bismarck's birthday.

Eichendorff with one of his verses inscribed on the plinth. Here you can stop for a while to enjoy the panorama of the castle, Königstuhl, Old Town and river Neckar. A small kiosk at the crossing of the paths sells refreshing drinks.

Above the path, and as far as Liselotteplatz, exotic plants, bushes and trees such as cork oak, jasmine, broom and the indigo bush have been planted. In spring and summer they spread a wonderful fragrance. Further on too you will be surprised again and again by Mediterranean plants and trees in the gardens along the way. It seems unusual for pomegranate, almond and lemon trees, bamboo, pines and palms to be thriving here, but this slope is one of the warmest places in Germany. Its south-facing aspect, its steep gradient of up to 45 degrees and the warming effect of downslope winds create special

I LOST MY HEART IN HEIDELBERG

The catchy tune that Fred Raymond composed in 1927 for lyrics by Fritz Löhner-Beda and Ernst Neubach is just one example of many songs and poems about Heidelberg. In 1800 Friedrich Hölderlin hailed Heidelberg in an ode as "the most beautiful city in all the fatherland", in 1855 Joseph von Eichendorff sang of his arrival in Heidelberg, and in 1854 Joseph Victor von Scheffel celebrated the town in his student song "Old Heidelberg, thou city fine, …None compares with thee", while Kurt Tucholsky parodied them all and Heidelberg's reputation: "the loveliest place that here on earth is mine, Heidelberg in Vienna on the Rhine". Few cities have been praised in song as much as Heidelberg.

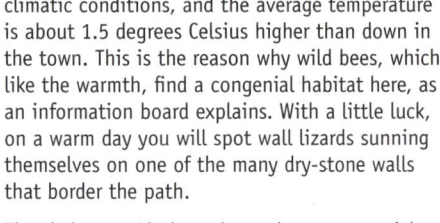

climatic conditions, and the average temperature is about 1.5 degrees Celsius higher than down in the town. This is the reason why wild bees, which like the warmth, find a congenial habitat here, as an information board explains. With a little luck, on a warm day you will spot wall lizards sunning themselves on one of the many dry-stone walls that border the path.

The shelter on *Liselotteplatz*, where a memorial stone commemorates Liselotte von der Pfalz, the sister-in-law of King Louis XIV of France, is especially popular as a place to stop for younger walkers, as there is a playground. You can work out what has changed in the panorama of Heidelberg since Matthäus Merian made his famous copperplate engraving in 1820 by studying the information board at the *Merianausblick*.

Before descending, continue to the *Hölderlin-Anlage*, a beautiful garden with a memorial to the poet Hölderlin on the spot where the hamlet of Dagersbach and its church once stood.

The path down passes between mossy old walls on the narrow *Schlangenweg*, which snakes down the slope, sometimes in the form of steps. In many places lookout points invite you to stop and admire the lovely view once again. At the end of the descent, cross Neuenheimer Landstraße and the Alte Brücke to return to the Old Town.

Strolling and Shopping

City Walk

University

Heidelberg by Night

Kurpfälzisches Museum

The Castle

3 Days In

Schwetzingen Palace

Philosophers' Walk

Strolling and Shopping

NEUENHEIM

The district where the Romans built a camp and which is mentioned for the first time in the year 765 in the Lorsch Codex is older than Heidelberg itself. Once a farming and fishing village, it was incorporated into the

town in 1891. Its idyllic character, its situation on the banks of the Neckar, proximity to the Old Town and many attractive dwellings make Neuenheim, with more than 13,000 residents, a sought-after place to live. It is best known for its university campus at Neuenheimer Feld. The Physikalisches Institut moved to Philosophenweg back in 1912, and since the 1950s scientific institutions, the university clinic, major research institutes and the Technologiepark have come to the west of Neuenheim.

STROLLING AND SHOPPING: ON AND AROUND THE HAUPTSTRASSE

Whether you plan to hunt through the outlets of well-known brand names or browse in little shops, in Heidelberg you will find appealing items for all tastes and in every price bracket.

The area that attracts most shoppers is the Old Town with its streets and alleys between Bis-

3 TIP To get your bearings in Heidelberg's shopping scene, download the App *MeinHeidelberg* free of charge from the AppStore or Android Market.

marckplatz and Kornmarkt. Heidelberg's number-one shopping street is the *Hauptstraße* (Main Street), which is described as one of Europe's

loveliest pedestrian zones thanks to its location at the heart of the Old Town. At Bismarckplatz the Darmstädter Hof, the town's biggest shopping centre,

and the four-storey Galeria Kaufhof department store mark the start of a shopping zone where all the famous names and brands of the national and international retail scene rub shoulders on a shopping street over one kilometre long.

If you prefer something more individual, walk through the side alleys and *Plöck*, which is parallel to the Hauptstraße, or *Untere Straße*. Here lots of little shops run by the owners sell unusual clothing, nice gifts and products from all around the world. In between them cafés and restaurants invite you to stop for a break, and when the sun shines you feel as if you were in the Mediterranean. Antique dealers and galleries have found

HEIDELBERG CONGRESS CENTER

Heidelberg Stadthalle was built in 1903 as a place for the citizens to assemble and celebrate. The charms of this sandstone building on the banks of the Neckar are its delicate Art Nouveau doors at the main entrance, elaborate sculptural decoration and holds 3,500 people. The new Heidelberg Congress Center is opened in the Bahnstadt quarter. Impressive architecture, narrative rooms,

a sustainable building concept will make Heidelberg, the city of science and knowledge, into a leading international destination for congresses.

www.heidelberg-congress.com/en

Have a break

To drink some hot chocolate or coffee and try home-made chocolate specialities or ice cream, go to **Chocolaterie St. Anna No 1.**

St. Anna Gasse 1

WESTSTADT

The Weststadt district is a good place to take a walk thanks to its heritage-listed villas, green courtyards, mature trees and buildings from the late 19th century, the period when the district was built on what used

to be farmland, at the time when the Badischer Bahnhof train station was constructed. This makes the Weststadt one of the finest examples of the urban planning of imperial Germany in the Wilhelmine years. The centre of the district is Wilhelmsplatz, the square next to the Church of St Boniface, where an arts market, the Kulturmarkt, is held every Saturday from 10am to 2 pm.
www.heidelberg.de/iba

a home in a street parallel to the Hauptstraße, Friedrich-Ebert-Anlage, which is worth strolling along if only for its fine historic townhouses.

If you walk across the Neckar bridge from Bismarckplatz, in good weather you will not only see the sunbathers on the grass by the riverbank but also reach the attractive district of *Neuenheim*. Here, around Brückenstraße, many small shops with individual service cover all aspects of daily life, selling fashion, jewellery, flowers, toys, books and much more. On Wednesdays and Saturdays a food market is held on Neuenheimer Marktplatz, where the late Gothic tower of old St John's Church can be seen.

Have a break

When the sun shines, **Bar Centrale** on the marketplace puts its chairs and tables outside so that guests can drink an espresso or eat a snack away from the crowds of tourists.
Ladenburger Straße 17

Schwetzingen Palace

ORIGINS OF THE PALACE

In 1350 a small moated castle was built on this site. Over the centuries it was rebuilt and destroyed several times. It owes its present Baroque appearance to Prince Elector Johann Wilhelm (1658–1716), who made it into a palace with three wings around a court of honour. When the summer residence of the court was moved from Mannheim to Schwetzingen under Elector Carl Philipp (1661–1741), the golden age of the palace began. His successor Carl Theodor (1724–99) extended Schloss Schwetzingen, built the court theatre and had the gardens newly laid out. Today the palace is owned by the federal state of Baden-Württemberg.

THE PRINCE ELECTORS' SUMMER RESIDENCE – SCHWETZINGEN PALACE

A visit to this Baroque palace ensemble takes you to a magnificent garden, a cultural heritage site of European significance.

Before you stroll through the palace garden, take time to visit the former state rooms and living apartments of the prince electors, which are furnished with authentic 18th-century items. On the courtyard side are the single-storey curved buildings called the Zirkelbauten, which were used for the court's games, concerts and balls.

Adjoining the North Zirkelbau and Orangery is the court theatre, built by Nicolas de Pigage. It was the first theatre in Germany to have tiered seating.

The palace gardens, among the most beautiful in Germany, are a masterpiece of late Baroque garden design. The front section was designed by the architect Nicolas de Pigage in the style of a French Baroque garden, while Friedrich Ludwig von Sckell, who created the rear section, took his inspiration from English landscape parks. The existence side by side of two completely different styles makes a walk through the gardens particularly enjoyable.

PRINCE ELECTORS

The title of "prince elector" ("Kurfürst") was held by those princes of the Holy Roman Empire who from the 13th century had the right to elect the king of the Germans. This right gave the prince electors a leading position in the empire. The electoral college consisted initially of seven, later of nine electors. They included the counts palatinate of the Rhine, whose seat was in Heidelberg for centuries and who had electoral rights because they were considered to be of particularly high status, as their territory lay in the area of the old Frankish kingdom.

The palace terrace commands a wonderful view of the strictly geometrical French-style Baroque garden, which is aligned with the central axis of the palace. A broad path that leads to the circular central parterre and the Arion Fountain emphasises this symmetry. To the right and left in parterres and bosquets are sculptures, small ponds, fountains and temples. The Natural Theatre, used for small-scale outdoor performances, is picturesquely integrated into the garden in a grotto. In the background the circular Temple of Apollo rises on a small mound, with a depiction of the god of the arts holding his lyre. Continue a little way to the

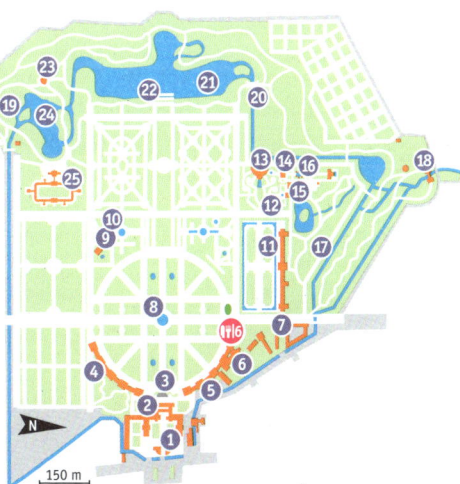

1 Court of honour with guard building, main entrance
2 Main palace building
3 Palace terrace
4 South Zirkelbau
5 North Zirkelbau
6 Rococo theatre
7 Invalids' barracks
8 Arion Fountain
9 Temple of Minerva and triton fountain
10 Avenue of urns with Lycian Apollo
11 Orangery and orangery garden
12 Natural Theatre
13 Temple of Apollo
14 Bathhouse and Wild Boar Grotto
15 Teahouse and Water Bell
16 Water-spouting birds
17 Arboretum and Baroque gates
18 Roman water fort with aqueduct
19 English Garden
20 Chinese Bridge
21 Great Pond
22 Rhine and Danube river gods
23 Temple of Mercury
24 Mosque pond
25 Mosque and Turkish Garden

SCHWETZINGEN SWR FESTIVAL

More than 70 years Schloss Schwetzingen has provided a stage for classical music from April to June. For four weeks under varying mottos varied programme includes a total of 50 concerts (some of them held in churches in the nearby city of Speyer) and two opera productions. In the historic court theatre an opera is usually staged by a well-known opera house, and a newly commissioned work or an unknown opera from the Baroque or Classical period is given a premiere. Established artists and talented young musicians present concerts of chamber and orchestral music, piano and lieder evenings, all of them broadcast by SWR2 radio. With some 550 radio broadcasts per year worldwide, the festival is also the biggest radio festival of classical music.

www.swr.de/swrclassic/ schwetzinger-festspiele/ index.html

Bathhouse, a private refuge for the prince elector where an oval room at the centre is decorated by a ceiling painting of the goddess Aurora, and take a look at the fountain with birds spouting water in the garden in front of it.

From the palace you can see the large lake at the end of the gardens. It is adorned by the gods of the rivers Rhine and Danube on the steps. If you walk over the Chinese Bridge you pass the lake and reach the English Garden, which lies to the west and northwest. The majestic artificial ruin that rises in the landscape is the Temple of Mercury. From its upper floor there is a wonderful view across the lake to the Red Mosque, which was not intended to be an Islamic place of worship but to express the principle of tolerance towards all the religions and cultures of the world. This domed building with its minarets can be seen above the water of the mosque lake, with the Turkish Garden and a large ambulatory with prayer niches carved in wood and pavilions.

▲ *Schloss (Rhein-NeckarBus 717 towards Speyer) www.schloss-schwetzingen.de/en/visitor-information/*

Have a break
Enjoy the princely surroundings of the **Schloss-restaurant Schwetzingen** inside the North Zirkelbau or on the terrace in front of it. *www.schlossrestaurant-schwetzingen.de*

Kurpfälzisches Museum

ZOO

A trip to Heidelberg Zoo, which was founded in 1934 by the Nobel laureate Carl Bosch and the ornithologist Otto Fehringer, is a popular outing for the whole family. According to the motto "see life live" visitors can get up close to impressive lions, tigers and bears amongst fine old trees, watch South American sea lions doing their tricks, admire the flight of giant sea eagles

and discover shyer animals such as snakes, toads and hedgehogs at the midday demonstration. Among the highlights are the extensive elephant compound and the new elephant house, in which the first group of young male elephants in a German zoo, consisting of four lively young bulls, is at home.

Tiergartenstraße 3
▲ *Zoo*
www.zoo-heidelberg.de

CENTURIES OF HISTORY – KURPFÄLZISCHES MUSEUM

A visit to the old Palais Morass immerses you deeply in the history of what used to be the Electoral Palatinate. You can make the acquaintance of the prince electors and their wives and admire the magnificence of their court life.

It is owing to the French émigré Charles de Graimberg and his extensive collection of paintings, prints, documents, coins, weapons, porcelain, sculptures and architectural fragments that Heidelberg possesses such an interesting museum today. After his death the town bought the collection in 1879, and from 1908 put it on display in the Baroque palais of Philipp Morass, a law professor. Thanks to archaeological finds, generous donations and purchases, visitors can take a historical trip from the earliest times to the 20th century.

Exciting discoveries await on a circuit of the museum, even though visitors may sometimes think they have lost their bearings as they follow a complicated path through the building and its wings.

Surprising artistic highlights keep appearing, from Tilman Riemenschneider's *Altar of the Apostles* dating from 1509, a tondo by Lucas Cranach the Elder depicting *Adam and Eve at the Fall of Man* (1525) and a *Madonna and Child* by Rogier van der Weyden (painted on wood, c 1455) to an opulently laid dinner table with a 72-piece silver service from Strasbourg that belonged to Elisabeth Augusta (1721–94), the last electoral princess. Reception and living rooms entirely fitted with period furniture, porcelain and paintings convey an impression of the life of the periods represented, and a gallery of dynastic paintings in the entrance area, with life-size portraits of Friedrich V and his consort Elizabeth Stuart, a portrait of Liselotte von der Pfalz in old age and a likeness of the court jester Perkeo, bring the history of the now-vanished Electoral Palatinate back to life.

To find out about the age of the bourgeoisie and the story of Heidelberg after 1800, take a look at the exhibition on Heidelberg in the Romantic age and the later 19th century on the ground floor.

Individual works and series from the prints collection show how the castle and town were depicted in the Romantic era. Fans of Dutch painting will be delighted by the Posselt Collection, which presents some 150 portraits, landscapes, genre scenes and still-lifes on wine-red walls.

BOTANICAL GARDEN

Founded in 1593 as the hortus medicus of the university, a garden for healing plants, the Botanischer Garten in Neuenheimer Feld is not only a place of relaxation where visitors come to stroll. It is used for scientific research and teaching, as a place where species threatened with extinc-

tion can be protected and as a place for public education. About 10,000 kinds of plants are cultivated in the hothouses and out in the open. The most significant collections are the orchids and bromeliads, as well as the currently largest European collection of dry plants from Madagascar.

Im Neuenheimer Feld 340 (Neuenheim)
▲ *Botanischer Garten botgart.hip. uni-heidelberg.de*

STIFT NEUBURG

Go back in time on a visit to the historic Stift Neuburg, a Benedictine Abbey which was a favourite rendezvous of the Romantics after its dissolution in 1804. Where Carl Maria von Weber was inspired to compose his opera *Der Freischütz*, and where Schlegel, Brentano, Görres and Rilke admired the abbey's beautiful site on a slope amid green meadows between Neuenheim and Ziegelhausen, since 1927 there has once again been a community of Benedictine monks. Today visitors can find a retreat in the monastery guesthouse for a few days, buy farm produce in the shop or try the monks' beer in the lovely beer garden.

Stiftweg 2-4 (Ziegelhausen),
▲ *Stift Neuburg*
www.klosterhof-neuburg.de

To go back to the early days of humanity, descend to the cellar, where a tour of the archaeological department begins with a copy of the lower jaw of Homo heidelbergensis (➤ p. 64). Here dioramas recreate the everyday life of a Neolithic family. Finds from excavations, the reconstruction of the Heidelberg Mithraeum and a Roman dining room tell the story of life in a Roman province. In the room with finds from excavations on Kornmarkt, a reconstructed kitchen with a hearth and furniture depicts life in Heidelberg around the year 1600. The lapidarium, a collection of stones related to the town's history with medieval epitaphs, the original sculptures from the Alte Brücke, the figure of Hercules from the well on the marketplace and other items, has found its place in the massive cellar vaults.

Hauptstraße 97
▲ *Kongresshaus/Stadthalle, Universitätsplatz, Peterskirche*
www.museum-heidelberg.de

Have a break

After all this art and history, the **restaurant** in the charming museum courtyard offers a welcome break with Italian food.
Hauptstraße 97
www.museum-heidelberg.de

Accommodation, Going Out, Tips and Addresses

Hotels

SKYLABS

SKYLABS, an ultra-low-energy building that provides approximately 19,500 square metres of space for research and laboratories, lies in the middle of the new technology campus of the Bahnstadt district. Its two five-storey buildings and a nine-storey tower with projecting upper floors make it stand out from its surroundings as a conspicuous symbol of pioneering connections between science

and business. As a new quarter of science-based high-tech companies, the campus has central facilities in order to enable companies from the biotechnology and pharmacology sectors to complete pre-clinical tests.

www.sky-labs.de

LOW BUDGET

● **HOTEL GARNI AM KORNMARKT****
Kornmarkt 7 (Old Town)
▲ Bergbahn/Rathaus
www.hotelamkornmarkt.de

Pleasant little hotel with a wonderful red Baroque façade right on Kornmarkt.

● **LOTTE –
THE BACKPACKERS**
Hostel Heidelberg
Burgweg 3 (Old Town)
▲ Bergbahn/Rathaus
www.lotte-heidelberg.de

Hostel with modern rooms in one of the town's oldest buildings, directly beneath the castle.

● **STEFFI'S HOSTEL HEIDELBERG**
Alte Eppelheimer Straße 50 (Bergheim)
▲ Hauptbahnhof
www.hostelheidelberg.de

Hostel welcomes backpackers from all over the world in a friendly and green oasis located just metres from the main station.

ECONOMY

● **ARTHOTEL HEIDELBERG****
Grabengasse 7 (Old Town)
▲ Universitätsplatz
www.arthotel.de

Near the university and in the heart of the Old Town, an architecturally appealing hotel thanks to its combination of a protected historic building with a modern addition.

● **BERGHEIM 41**
Hotel im Alten Hallenbad
Bergheimer Straße 41 (Bergheim)
▲ Bismarckplatz
www.bergheim41.de

This modern city hotel in the Altes Hallenbad, an old swimming pool complex mixing Art Nouveau and Classical styles, is close to Bismarckplatz and boasts a roof garden with a view of the castle.

● **HOLLÄNDER HOF***[S]
Neckarstaden 66 (Old Town)
▲ Marstallstraße
www.hollaender-hof.de

Romantic hotel with a superb view of the Alte Brücke, the Neckar and Philosophenweg.

● **HOTEL "CAFÉ FRISCH"**
Jahnstraße 34
(Neuenheim)
▲ Jahnstraße
www.cafe-frisch.de

Family-run accommodation
right by the Neckar near
the university clinic and
the research facilities in
Neuenheimer Feld, popular
for the in-house bakery.

● **MARRIOTT
HEIDELBERG**★★★★
Vangerowstraße 16
(Bergheim)
▲ Betriebshof
www.marriott.de

Business hotel on the
banks of the Neckar,
at the approach to the
town, close to Bahnstadt
and convenient for the
autobahn.

● **QUBE HOTEL
HEIDELBERG**
Bergheimer Straße 74
(Bergheim)
▲ Römerstraße
www.qube-hotel-heidelberg.de

Privately run design hotel
near the station with
an award-winning
restaurant.

SUPERIOR

● **HEIDELBERG
SUITES**★★★★★
Neuenheimer
Landstraße 12 (Old Town)
▲ Alte Brücke Nord
www.houseofhuetter.com/
heidelberg-suites

Near the university and
in the heart of the Old
Town, an architecturally
appealing hotel thanks
to its combination of a
protected historic building
with a modern addition.

● **VILLA
MARSTALL**★★★★⁺
Lauerstraße 1 (Old Town)
▲ Marstallstraße
www.villamarstall.de

Attractive hotel in a late
Classical townhouse in
the Old Town, right by the
Neckar with a view of the
castle, Alte Brücke and
Philosophenweg.

BAHNSTADT

Cities can change their
appearance quickly –
as demonstrated by
the new quarter that
was built on the site
of a former rail freight
yard between the
districts Weststadt and
Pfaffengrund. Here a
"City of Knowledge" was
being conceived, with
everything that scien-
tists need to live and
work. On an area of 116
hectares, larger than
Heidelberg's Old Town,
this new quarter makes
space available for
scientific work, accom-
modation, enjoying life,
art and culture. There is
housing for 6,500 peo-
ple and places of work
up to 6,000. The energy
planning also looks to
the future, as it will be
Europe's largest district
of sustainable "passive
buildings" with ultra-low
energy consumption.

www.heidelberg-
bahnstadt.de

Restaurants

HEIDELBERG SPECIALITIES

Apfelküchle:
pancakes with slices of apples, to which are added sugar and cinnamon or custard.

Buwespitzle:
(also called Schupf-nudeln): a mix of potato, egg, flour and butter, pressed into pasta shape and fried.

Handkäs mit Musik:
ripe sour-milk cheese marinated in chopped onions with vinegar, oil, caraway seeds, pepper and salt.

Kartäuserklösse:
a poor man's dish made of stale bread rolls soaked in milk with sugar and egg white, dipped in flour then fried and sprinkled with sugar and cinnamon.

● **DAS BOOTSHAUS**
Schurmanstraße 2 (Bergheim)
▲ Thibautstraße
www.dasbootshaus.com

The former boathouse of the Heidelberg rowing club has a sunny terrace with a direct view of the Neckar, where meals inspired by the Pacific region and Asia are served.

● **CHAMBAO**
Dreikönigstraße 1 (Old Town)
▲ Alte Brücke
www.chambao-heidelberg.de

Cosy Mediterranean restaurant right on the old bridge with glass kitchen and "sharing" offers!

● **HUGO WINE & DINE**
Rohrbacher Straße 47 (Weststadt)
▲ Hans-Böckler-Straße, Kaiserstraße
www.hugo-hd.de

The in-house wine shop is not the only reason to come to this restaurant with a Mediterranean atmosphere and a creative menu.

● **LE COQ**
Brückenstraße 17 (Neuenheim)
▲ Brückenstraße
www.lecoq-hd.de

A pleasant place with a casual atmosphere to spend an evening enjoying classic French food and more.

● **OSKAR**
Haspelgasse 5 (Old Town)
▲ Marstallstraße
www.oskar-hd.de

Here you can enjoy German and Mediterranean dishes with a glass of good wine.

● **PICCOLO MONDO**
Klingenteichstraße 6 (Altstadt)
▲ Peterskirche
www.piccolomondo-heidelberg.de
A wonderful place for lovers of Italian food.

Parsnip foam soup, blood-orange and chilli chutney – this restaurant serves vegetarian treats.

● **RESTAURANT ROMER**
Grabengasse 7 (Old Town)
▲ Universitätsplatz
www.arthotel.de

A combination of regional and international dishes in a nice surroundings.

● **RESTAURANT QUBE**
Bergheimer Straße 74 (Bergheim)
▲ Römerstraße
www.qube-hotel-heidelberg.de

Spoil yourself with imaginative herbal cuisine and top-class regional products!

● **RED – DIE GRÜNE KÜCHE**
Poststraße 42 (Bergheim)
www.red-diegruene-kueche.com

● **RESTAURANT TATI**
Bergheimer Straße 151 (Bergheim)
▲ Betriebshof
www.restaurant-tati.de

If you like French cuisine, here you will find a little patch of France.

● **SAME SAME**
Steingasse 3 (Old Town)
▲ Alte Brücke
www.sushiheidelberg.de

Tiny sushi bar for fans of raw fish.

HEIDELBERG SPECIALITIES

Kerscheplotzer or Kirschenmichel:
a bake of soaked bread rolls with eggs, sugar, butter, almonds, sweet cherries and cherry schnapps, eaten hot or cold with or without custard.

Maultaschen:
pasta filled with meat, spinach, onions and breadcrumbs.

Saumagen:
a mix of meat, bacon, onions, chestnuts, herbs and potatoes, cooked in a pig's stomach.

Verheierte:
a stew of meat broth with pieces of potato, spätzle noodles, onions and meat.

Cafés & Pubs

HEIDELBERG CALENDAR

DEC-FEB:
Winter in Schwetzingen
www.theaterheidelberg.de

FEB:
Adelante – Iberoameri-
can Theater Festival
www.adelante-festival.de
festival of cabaret and
other performing arts
www.karlstorbahnhof.de

APRIL:
Musikfestival Heidel-
berger Frühling
*www.heidelberger-
fruehling.de*

APRIL/MAY:
Heidelberger Stücke-
markt theatre festival
www.theaterheidelberg.de

JUNE:
Literature festival
www.heidellittage.de

Handschuhsheimer
Kerwe, a traditional fair
*www.tiefburg.de/
kerwe.htm*

● **CAFÉ GUNDEL**
Hauptstraße 212
(Old Town)
▲ Rathaus/Bergbahn
www.gundel-heidelberg.de

On the terrace with a view
of the castle you can try
out many different kinds
of cake.

● **CAFÉ KNÖSEL**
Untere Straße 37
(Old Town)
▲ Marstallstraße
◆ 8.30am-10pm
www.cafeknoesel-hd.de

This is the town's oldest
chocolaterie, a traditional
café since 1863, where the
Heidelberg "student kiss"
was invented.

● **CAFÉ ROSSI**
Rohrbacher Straße 4
(Old Town)
▲ Bismarckplatz
www.caferossi.de

A vibrant place that is
always full – on Bismarckplatz, where the large old
beer garden gives you a
holiday feeling.

● **CAFÉ SCHAFHEUTLE**
Hauptstraße 94
(Old Town)
▲ Peterskirche
www.cafe-schafheutle.de

Enjoy exquisite cakes and
biscuits or delicious ice
cream with a view of the
pedestrian zone or in the
pleasant garden.

● **CENNETO WEINBAR**
Da-Vinci-Straße 18
(Bahnstadt)
▲ Gadamerplatz
www.cenneto.com

Wine is best drunk in
company, you should
definitely try it out in this
beautiful wine bar!

● **COFFEE NERD**
Poststraße 18-20
(Old Town)
▲ Adenauerplatz
www.coffeenerd.de

A youthful coffee bar
with the obligatory racing
bike on the wall, providing
everything connected
with coffee.

● **KULTURBRAUEREI**
Leyergasse 6 (Old Town)
▲ Neckarmünzplatz
www.heidelberger-kultur-brauerei.de

In historic brewery buildings or in the leafy courtyard, enjoy roast pork, sauerbraten, schäufele or crispy fried duck, washed down with the beer brewed on site.

● **MORO CAFFÉ**
Hauptstraße 160
(Old Town)
▲ Universitätsplatz
www.facebook.com/CafeMoroAltstadt

It's a bit like being in the Mediterranean: you can drink espresso (or tea if your prefer) at leisure and eat some cake while watching what's happening on the street.

● **SCHMELZPUNKT**
Hauptstraße 90
(Old Town)
▲ Peterskirche
www.schmelzpunkt-heidelberg.de

If you like to let home-made ice-cream melt in your mouth or spoil

yourself with delicate chocolate creations, this is the right place.

● **VETTER'S ALT HEIDEL-BERGER BRAUHAUS**
Steingasse 9 (Old Town)
▲ Marstallstraße
www.brauhaus-vetter.de

Brewery in a guest house with its own kinds of beer and down-to-earth German cooking.

● **ZUM GÜLDENEN SCHAF**
Hauptstraße 115
(Old Town)
▲ Universitätsplatz
www.schaf-heidelberg.de

Old-established restaurant with an idyllic beer garden in the middle of the Old Town.

HEIDELBERG CALENDAR

JUNE/JULY/SEPT:
The castle illuminated
www.heidelberg-marketing.de

SUMMER:
Schlossfestspiele, theatre and opera festival
www.theaterheidelberg.de

SEPT:
Heidelberger Herbst, festival in the Old Town
www.heidelberg-marketing.de

Enjoy Jazz
www.enjoyjazz.de

OCT:
KinderTheaterFestival Heidelberg

NOV:
Internationales Filmfestival Mannheim-Heidelberg
www.iffmh.de

DEC:
Christmas Market, Christmas on Ice on Karlsplatz
www.heidelberg-marketing.de

Bars & Nightlife

HEIDELBERG'S VITAL STATISTICS

Heidelberg has a population of more than 160,000 and is situated near to the point where the Neckar flows into the Rhine. The city boundaries enclose an area of about 109 square kilometres, of which almost 30 per cent, or

32.2 square kilometres, are built up and 44.2 square kilometres are woodland. The extent of the city area is approx. 13 kilometres east-west and approx. 10 kilometres north-south.

Heidelberg lies in the Upper Rhine Valley on the left bank of the Neckar in one the warmest regions in Germany, and is divided into 15 districts. Its highest point at 586 metres is the Königstuhl, and the lowest point on the river bank at Neckarsteinach lies 116 metres above sea level.

● **BAR D'AIX EN PROVENCE**
Bergstraße 1 (Neuenheim)
▲ Brückenstraße
www.bardaix-heidelberg.de

Small bar with a French atmosphere off the tourist trail.

● **BENT BAR**
Leyergasse 2 (Old Town)
▲ Neckarmünzplatz
www.bentbar.de

An elegant bar in 60s and 70s style away from the bustle of the Old Town, a good place for sipping a cocktail.

● **CAVE 54**
Krämergasse 2 (Old Town)
▲ Rathaus/Bergbahn
www.cave54.de

In Germany's oldest student club you meet people of all ages who come to dance or for concerts of jazz, blues or rock music.

● **COCKTAIL CAFÉ REGIE**
Theaterstraße 2
(Old Town)
▲ Kongresshaus
www.regie-heidelberg.de

These cocktail specialists will serve you 180 different cocktails, cool soft drinks and more to enjoy on the biggest outdoor terrace in the Old Town of Heidelberg.

● **HEMINGWAY'S**
Fahrtgasse 1
▲ Bismarckplatz
www.hemingways-heidelberg.de

Here you can follow in the footsteps of Ernest Hemingway, relaxing with Caribbean cocktails.

● **JINX**
Untere Straße 20
(Old Town)
www.facebook.com/jinx.heidelberg

A cocktail bar with a club atmosphere where you can relax, celebrate and enjoy a drink.

● **KAISER**
Untere Straße 30
(Old Town)
▲ Alte Brücke
www.kaiser-heidelberg.de

In the evening this cool bar changes into a dance bar the whole night.

Print Media Lounge

Alongside Mannheim and Ludwigshafen, Heidelberg is one of the three main centres of the Rhine-Neckar conurbation, which has approx. 2.4 million inhabitants. The city itself has Germany's oldest university and a population of some 38,000 students at four institutions of higher education.

Heidelberg is also the seat of the Akademie der Wissenschaften (Academy of Sciences) and several major research institutes such as the European Molecular Biology Laboratory (EMBL), the German Cancer Research Centre (DKFZ) and five Max Planck Institutes. The technology park, home to over 80 companies and research institutes, is among the leading centres of biotechnology in Germany and worldwide. Heidelberg is also a dynamic business centre where well-known firms such as Heidelberger Druckmaschinen AG, HeidelbergCement, ABB Stotz, SAP, SAS Institute and the important academic publisher Springer Nature are based.

● **ORANGE BAR**
Ingrimstraße 26 (Old Town)
▲ Alte Brücke Nord
www.orange-heidelberg.de

An oasis in the Old Town with the atmosphere of a living room, and the ideal spot for a glass of wine or more.

● **PIER 4**
Neckarstaden 25 (Old Town)
▲ St. Vincentius-Krankenhaus
pier4-heidelberg.de

This swimming location on the Neckar quays below the Stadthalle is recommended for a drink with a wonderful view of the river.

● **TANGENTE**
Kettengasse 23 (Old Town)
▲ Universitätsplatz
www.tangente-hd.de

A small club where you can dance to the sounds of soul, funk, r'n'b, house & disco.

● **TONIQ**
Hauptstraße 1 (in Darmstädter Hof/Old Town)
▲ Bismarckplatz
www.toniq-club.de

Club in the old town for everyone who likes to dance and party.

Spas & Fitness

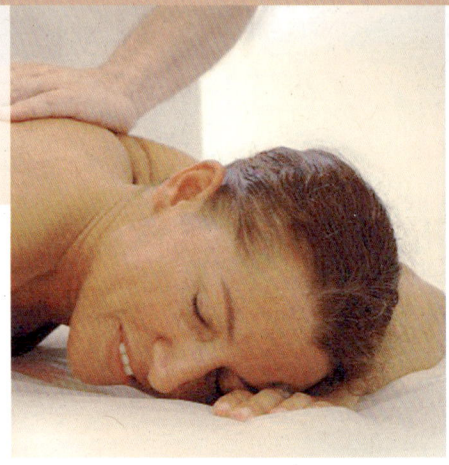

PRINT MEDIA ACADEMY

When you leave the station, a 13-metre-high sculpture of a horse made of stainless steel and aluminium catches the eye. The S-Printing Horse by the sculptor Jürgen Goertz is the world's largest sculpture of a horse and symbolises the different processes in a printing works on the square in front of the communication and

know-how centre of Heidelberger Druckmaschinen AG, a manufacturer of printing machines. The 12-storey glass cube houses offices and is used for training courses that range from machine training to management seminars. The Print Media Academy also serves as a venue for congresses and conferences and has an event location on the 12th floor.

● HALLENBAD KÖPFEL
Stiftweg 32 (Ziegelhausen)
▲ Köpfel
www.heidelberger-stadtwerke.de

Indoor swimming pool with a sauna in the Sportzentrum Ziegelhausen, which has a warm bathing day twice a week with 30° C water temperature.

● MASSAGE ROYAL
Friedrich-Ebert-Anlage 12 (Bergheim)
▲ Adenauerplatz, Poststraße
www.massagesalon heidelberg.de

With a whole-body massage with aromatic oils, an African baobab massage or a foot reflexology massage, you can definitely relax here.

● PANORAMA SPA CLUB
In the Europäischer Hof
Friedrich-Ebert-Anlage 1 (Old Town)
▲ Adenauerplatz, Poststraße
www.europaeischerhof.com

A spa above the roofs of Heidelberg with a sauna, sanarium, steam bath, sun beds, outdoor terrace and state-of-the-art equipment for a workout.

● SALZRAUM HEIDELBERG
Rohrbacher Straße 20 (Weststadt)
▲ Adenauerplatz, Poststraße
www.salzraum-heidelberg.de

The "salt room", which consists entirely of natural crystal salt, truly gives a feeling of well-being, not only for the respiratory system and the skin. You can also relax on the jade massage beds.

An authentic Thai massage to tone you up and enjoy the atmosphere and the soothing effect of a little rest.

● **THERMALBAD**
Vangerowstraße 4 (Bergheim)
▲ Volkshochschule
www.swhd.de/thermalbad

You can swim with flair, with a view of the Odenwald and in a beautiful location under large old trees in the traditional thermal baths from 1939, faithfully renovated.

● **ORCHID THAI-MASSAGE**
Bergheimer Straße 125 (Bergheim)
▲ Betriebshof
www.orchid-heidelberg.com

● **SABEI-SABEI-THAI-MASSAGE**
In the Marriott Hotel
Vangerowstraße 16
▲ Betriebshof
www.sabaisabaiheidelberg.de

Here you can relax in the spa zone with a view of the Neckar, get fit on the training equipment in the gym area, or spoil yourself with a massage or cosmetic treatment.

BERGFRIEDHOF

For a walk or to meditate in peace, the old cemetery called Bergfriedhof on the site of a former vineyard on the border between the Weststadt and Südstadt is always worth visiting. When the garden designer Johann Christian Metzger laid out this non-denominational cemetery in 1844, he planned to retain existing features of the topography and a natural appearance of the site. Today visitors can walk around an area of 17 hectares with a network of winding paths totalling 23 kilometres and more than 18 terraces among a rich variety of vegetation, including ancient trees and shrubs. The famous people who are buried here include Friedrich Ebert (German president during the Weimar

Republic), the composer and conductor Wilhelm Furtwängler, the scientists Carl Bosch and Robert Bunsen, and the poet Hilde Domin.

Steigerweg 20,
▲ *West-/Südstadt, Bergfriedhof*

Culture

HEIDELBERGER FRÜHLING

Every year the international Heidelberger Frühling music festival in March and April stages approximately 100 events, inviting connoisseurs and newcomers alike to enter the world of classical

music with world stars and young artists. The Heidelberger Frühling is characterised by its aim to be a mediator of music, to get people to think about the impact of music on society and their own lives. For this reason the festival has a different overall motto each year, which is discussed more deeply in lectures, workshops and talks with artists, and thus enables the performers and the audiences to engage in an informal exchange of views. In addition to major concert evenings in festive surroundings, it is above all projects such as the string quartet festival and the Festival Academy that constitute the appeal of this event.

www.heidelberger-fruehling.de

MUSIC

● **COLLEGIUM MUSICUM**
Augustinergasse 7
(Old Town)
▲ Universitätsplatz
www.uni-heidelberg.de

As representatives of the quality of the university music, this orchestra and choir stage regular concerts and are a fixture in the musical life of Heidelberg.

● **KONGRESSHAUS STADTHALLE HEIDELBERG**
Neckarstaden 24
(Old Town)
▲ Kongresshaus
www.heidelberg-kongresshaus.de

A great variety of performances are staged in the main auditorium: the programme ranges from classical concerts and pop or rock events to cabaret and comedy.

● **JAZZHAUS HEIDELBERG**
Leyergasse 6 (Old Town)
▲ Neckarmünz-Platz
www.jazzhaus-heidelberg.de

In the vaults of the old cellar, some 150 concerts a year are held, with an emphasis on modern jazz, but also evenings of soul, blues, rhythm'n blues, rock and chansons.

● **PHILHARMONISCHES ORCHESTER HEIDELBERG**
Theaterstraße 10
(Old Town)
▲ Peterskirche, Universitätsplatz
Tickets and information:
tel. 06221/582000,
tickets@theater.heidelberg.de
www.theaterheidelberg.de

The general director of music, Elias Grandy, takes the opera and concert orchestra on a musical journey to all points of the compass, and presents internationally famous artists.

● **SINFONIEORCHESTER TONART**
Heinrich-Fuchs-Straße 22
Programme:
www.tonart-heidelberg.de

This ensemble of students and amateurs with many years of experience plays varied programmes to a high standard under its conductor Knud Jansen.

THEATRE & CABARET

● **AHA-UNTERWEGS-THEATER**
HebelHalle/Hebelstraße 9 (Weststadt)
▲ Rudolf-Diesel-Straße
www.unterwegstheater.de

This company based in the HebelHalle moves between the genres of dance, acrobatics and drama, and aims to express itself in its own inimitable style.

● **ROMANISCHER KELLER**
Seminarstraße 3 / corner of Kettengasse (Old Town)
▲ Universitätsplatz
www.uni-heidelberg.de/rose/einrichtungen/romankeller

The university theatre, a forum for student drama and the independent theatre scene and venue for cabaret, music and culture.

THE STUDENT PRINCE

The play *Alt-Heidelberg*, based on a story by Wilhelm Meyer-Förster, premiered in Berlin in 1901 and made Heidelberg famous all over the world. Derided by Kurt Tucholsky as a soulful melodrama, in the first half of the 20th century it was among the most-performed plays and was filmed several times. The story of the heir to the throne Karl-Heinrich, a student in a Heidelberg fraternity who falls in love below his station with the pretty innkeeper's daughter Kathie but has to sacrifice his love for raison d'état, was the model for the Broadway musical by Sigmund Romberg that was a smash hit from 1924 under the title *The Student Prince* and was often performed at the Heidelberger Schlossfestspiele.

Culture

HEIDELBERGER SCHLOSSFESTSPIELE

Could there be a more beautiful backdrop for plays than the world-famous ruined castle? If you would like to experience this for yourself, book tickets for the Schlossfestspiele (castle festival) in summer. Established in 1926 with a performance of *Midsummer Night's Dream*, the festival came to an end during the Weimar Republic and was not revived until 1974 with the old Heidelberg musical *The Student Prince*. Today it is run by Heidelberg's mu-

nicipal theatre, and puts on drama and opera in a variety of venues in the castle. Added to this is an exciting and diverse programme of concerts that encompasses lively hits from operetta, favourite Italian opera arias, classic music from the movies and summer concerts.

www.heidelberger-schlossfestspiele.de

● TAETER-THEATER
Bergheimer Straße 147
▲ Hauptbahnhof, Betriebshof
www.taeter-theater.de

The repertoire of this theatre, where director Wolfgang Graczol stages dramas in collaboration with amateur actors, ranges from classical to contemporary pieces.

● THEATER UND ORCHESTER HEIDELBERG/ JUNGES THEATER
Theaterstraße 10 (Old Town)
Tickets and information: tickets@theater.heidelberg.de
www.theaterheidelberg.de

A theatre with five fields of activity: opera, concerts, drama, dance, and children's and youth theatre in a newly renovated old theatre, in the Zwinger and at other venues. Under the direction of Holger Schultze its programme combines the traditional and the modern. Thanks to the Dance Company Nanine Linning/Theater Heidelberg, the Theater und Orchester Heidelberg now has its own dance ensemble again.

● TIKK – THEATER IM KULTURHAUS KARLSTORBAHNHOF
Am Karlstor 1 (Old Town)
▲ S-Bahnhof Altstadt
www.karlstorbahnhof.de

Whether theatre, dance, cabaret or readings, the stage of this arts centre has a wide-ranging programme covering different genres.

● ZIMMERTHEATER HEIDELBERG
Hauptstraße 118 (Old Town)
▲ Universitätsplatz
www.zimmertheaterhd.de

For more than 60 years this privately run theatre with just 93 seats in picturesque backyard premises has been present-

ing contemporary drama on a studio stage, including premieres of new works.

CINEMAS

● **DIE KAMERA**
Brückenstraße 26
(Neuenheim)
▲ Brückenstraße
www.gloria-kamera-kinos.de

Small arthouse cinema screening films out of the mainstream.

● **GLORIA & GLORIETTE**
Hauptstraße 146
(Old Town)
▲ Peterskirche,
Universitätsplatz

This arthouse cinema often shows films in the original language.

● **KARLSTORKINO**
Am Karlstor 1, (Old Town)
▲ S-Bahnhof Altstadt,
Heidelberg Altstadt
www.karlstorkino.de

An ambitious, non-commercial movie programme that aims to widen the horizons of its audience for films and film history.

● **KINO IM MARSTALCAFÉ**
Marstallhof 1 (Old Town)
▲ Kongresshaus
www.stw.uni-heidelberg.de/de/node/360

Student atmosphere: comedies and movies for cinéastes, films that are high-brow and low-brow, moving and thrilling.

GALERIE EDITION STAECK

Among the many galleries in Heidelberg, the best-known is surely that of the graphic artist Klaus Staeck (born 1938), who since 1986 has been visiting professor at the Academy of Art in Düsseldorf and since 2006 president of the Academy of Arts in Berlin. Founded by Staeck in 1965 under the name Edition Tangente, it exhibits 20th-century works as well as postcards, posters, objects and books by the artist himself.

His satirical posters and classic works of political art, and his critical attitude to politics, have reached a wide audience through his mass sales of postcards.

Ingrimstraße 3
▲ *Alte Brücke*
www.edition-staeck.de

SERVICE

Museums

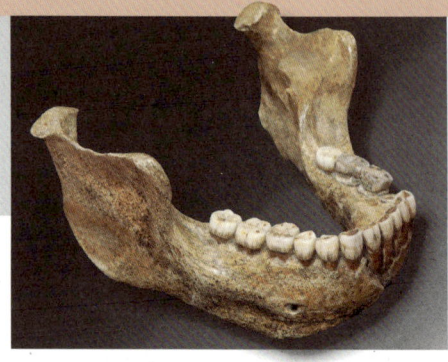

● ANTIKENMUSEUM UND ABGUSS-SAMMLUNG
➤ p. 22

● CARL BOSCH MUSEUM
Schloss-Wolfsbrunnen-weg 4
▲ Hausackerweg
◆ Fri-Wed 10am-5pm
www.carl-bosch-museum.de

Fascinating insights into the life and discoveries of the Nobel laureate Carl Bosch.

APOTHEKENMUSEUM
➤ p. 32

● DOKUMENTATIONS- UND KULTURZEN-TRUM DEUTSCHER SINTI UND ROMA
Bremeneckgasse 2
▲ Rathaus/Bergbahn
◆ Tue 9.30am-6.45pm, Wed-Fri 9.30am-4.30pm, Sat-Sun 11am-4.30pm
www.dokuzentrum.sintiun-droma.de/en

The most important place of memorial in Germany for the victims of the Porajmos, the persecution of Sinti and Roma by the Nazis.

HOMO HEIDELBERGENSIS

The collection of the Institute for Earth Science contains one of the most important finds in the history of humanity: the 600,000-year-old lower jaw of Homo heidelbergensis. "Heidelberg man" owes his name to the place where the find was made, in a sand pit near Mauer close to Heidelberg. In evolutionary terms Homo heidelbergensis developed from Homo erectus, and evolved further to become Neanderthal man about 200,000 years ago in Europe. From parts of skeletons that have been found it is known that Heidelberg man was a successful hunter in Europe and parts of Africa, living mainly by hunting big game.

Institut für Geowissenschaften,
Im Neuenheimer Feld 234-236 (Neuenheim)
◆ Mon-Fri 9am-5pm, www.geow.uni-heidelberg.de

● HEIDELBERGER KUNSTVEREIN
Hauptstraße 97 (Old Town)
▲ Peterskirche
◆ Tue-Sun 11am-6pm
www.hdkv.de

Contemporary art in a large bright gallery on three floors.

● KURPFÄLZISCHES MUSEUM
➤ p. 45 ff.

● MUSEUM HAUS CAJETH
Haspelgasse 12 (Old Town)
▲ Marstallstraße
◆ Mon-Fri 11am-5pm, Sat noon-3pm
www.cajeth.de

Museum with paintings by unknown artists.

● SAMMLUNG DES ÄGYPTOLOGISCHEN INSTITUTS
Marstallhof 6 (1st floor/Old Town)
▲ Marstallstraße
◆ on request
www.uni-heidelberg.de

The collection of the institute for Egyptology explains the life of the ancient Egyptians and their religious beliefs.

● STIFTUNG REICHSPRÄSIDENT-FRIEDRICH-EBERT-GEDENKSTÄTTE
➤ p. 15

● STUHLMUSEUM
Plöck 16 (Old Town)
▲ Bismarckplatz
◆ Mon-Fri 9am-noon, 1-3.30pm
www.wohnungslosenhilfe-stadtmission.de/stuhl-museum_heidelberg.php

The chair museum illuminates the subject of seating.

● TEXTILSAMMLUNG MAX BERK/KUR-PFÄLZISCHES MUSEUM
Brahmsstraße 8 (Ziegelhausen)
▲ Brahmsstraße
◆ Tue-Sun 10am-6pm
www.museum-heidelberg.de

In addition to a collection of women's fashion and production machinery this museum explains production methods and the use of various kinds of animal and plant fibres in textiles.

● VÖLKERKUNDE-MUSEUM
Hauptstraße 235 (Palais Weimar)
▲ Neckarmünzplatz, Altstadt rail station
◆ Wed-Sat 2-6pm, Sun 11am-6pm
www.voelkerkunde museum-vpst.de

Works of art and ethno-graphic items from Asia, Africa and Oceania, as well as changing exhibitions about the art and culture of various regions.

SAMMLUNG PRINZHORN

To collect works produced in psychiatric clinics was a most extraordinary idea in the early 20th century. Because the doctor and art historian Hans Prinzhorn hoped to be able to use the paintings for diagnosis and to find an elementary, undistorted way of accessing art, he collected the works of his psychiatric patients and published them in 1922 in *Artistry of the Mentally Ill*. In his life-time the medical profession rejected his ideas, but today Prinzhorn is regarded as a pioneer of this interdisciplinary approach. Artists such as Paul Klee, Max Ernst and Pablo Picasso were fascinated and inspired by these "works of mad-ness". The power and beauty of the pictures can be appreciated today in the lecture-theatre building of what was once the neurologi-cal clinic, where parts of the collection, which now consists of 5,000 works, are on show in changing exhibitions.

Psychiatrische Universitätsklinik Voßstraße 4 (Bergheim)
▲ *Thibautstraße*
◆ *Opening times during exhibitions:*
Tue, Thu-Sun 11am-5pm, Wed 11am-8pm
www.prinzhorn.ukl-hd.de

Shopping

A STUDENT KISS FROM HEIDELBERG

Once you have tried this delicious confection made from chocolate, nougat and waffle, you will not want to live without it. This must have been the sentiment of the young ladies who liked to meet in Café Knösel in the second half of the 19th century. As they were only allowed to go there accompanied by eagle-eyed governesses, the students who were present could do no more than cast hopeful glances at them. This gave the humorous chocolatier and pastry cook Fridolin Knösel the brilliant idea of creating an especially exquisite chocolate treat, which could be presented under the name "student kiss" as a token of admiration without arousing the disapproval of the governesses. Knösel's student kiss has now become the city's sweet emblem.

● **FARBENREICH**
Plöck 75 (Old Town)
▲ Peterskirche
www.facebook.com/Farben-reichHeidelberg

Fabrics and wallpaper in retro design, modern jewellery, bags, crockery, cards, baskets, boxes and knick-knacks – here you can rummage through lots of colourful items.

● **HEIDELBERGER ZUCKERLADEN**
Plöck 52 (Old Town)
▲ Peterskirche
www.heidelberger-zuckerladen.de

If you have a sweet tooth, this place is heaven. Everything from lollipops, nougat and marzipan to wine gums, all in old-fashioned jars.

● **HOLGERSONS**
Theaterstraße 2 a (Old Town)
▲ Kongresshaus
www.holgersons.de

Come here to buy things of beauty for everyday use, or to drink a cup of coffee in the sunshine.

● **L'EPICERIE – MAGALI SOULIE**
Hauptstraße 35 (backyard/Old Town)
▲ Bismarckplatz
www.lepicerie.de

If you would like to pick up oil, vinegar, spices or unusual flavours of chocolate, the selection here is wide.

● **MUSIKZIMMER HEIDELBERG**
Untere Straße 10 (Old Town)
▲ Marstallstraße
www.facebook.com/musikzimmer.heidelberg

A small store with a big selection, especially vinyl.

● **PRALINENMANU-
FAKTUR VORBACH
HEIDELBERG**
Hauptstraße 211
(Old Town)
▲ Rathaus/Bergbahn
◆ by telephone arrangement
0160/6229517
*www.vorbach-pralinenman-
ufaktur.sugartrends.com/de*

This manufactory of fine
chocolates sells truffles
with names like "Heidel-
berg love story" and
"castle mixture". Just the
place for self-indulgence.

● **TROLL SPIELZEUG**
Plöck 71 (Old Town)
▲ Friedrich-Ebert-Platz
*www.troll-heidelberg.
jimdofree.com*

Come here to find toys for
younger and older kids.

● **UNISHOP**
Augustinergasse 2
(Old Town)
▲ Universitätsplatz
www.unishop.uni-hd.de

Not only for students: here
you will find gifts as well as
lots of useful products for
student life, all of it bearing
the logo of the university.

● **WEINHAUS
C. FEHSER OHG**
Friedrich-Ebert-Anlage 26
(Old Town)
▲ Friedrich-Ebert-Platz
www.weinversand-fehser.de

Traditional family
company that stocks
a big range of inter-
national wines and
spirits.

**WINE FROM
HEIDELBERG**

Not only the wine vil-
lages on the Bergstraße
route, known as the
"German Riviera" thanks
to its mild climate, pro-
duce top wines. As the
famous giant barrel in
Heidelberg Castle shows,
wine has been made in
this area for a long time.
The district of Rohrbach
is thought to be one of
the oldest wine villages,
as it is mentioned in a
charter of Lorsch mon-
astery dating from 766
in connection with the
donation of a vineyard.
Due to the outstanding
conditions for making
wine in this small but
superb wine region, for
example Heidelberger
Dachsbuckel with its
Riesling vines, Heidel-
berger Dornenacker,
Heidelberger Herrenberg
and Heidelberger Son-
nenseite ob der Bruck,
a vineyard opposite the
castle at the foot of
Philosophenweg, various
sites regularly produce
vintages that win major
awards.

Addresses

EUROPEAN MOLE-CULAR BIOLOGY LABORATORY (EMBL)

The European Laboratory for Molecular Biology, which has its headquarters in Heidelberg, is one of the world's best-known research labs. It focusses on basic research in molecular biology, the development and transfer of new technologies, and training and services for scientists from all over the world. This research institute is operated by

20 European states, with Australia as an associate member. The EMBL has outposts in Cambridge, Grenoble, Hamburg and Rome. Some 85 independent research groups work at the EMBL on subjects covering the whole range of molecular biology.

www.embl.de

● **HEIDELBERG MARKETING GMBH**
Neuenheimer Landstraße 5
69120 Heidelberg
tel. 06221/5844444
www.heidelberg-marketing.de

● **TOURIST INFORMATI-ON AT THE MAIN RAIL STATION**
Willy-Brandt-Platz 1
tel. 06221/5844444

● **TOURIST INFORMATION AT THE CITY HALL (RATHAUS)**
Marktplatz

BY CAR: The Rhine-Neck-ar region is served by au-tobahn A5 and autobahn A6. There are direct exits to Heidelberg from the A5 and the A656.

BY RAIL: Heidelberg is linked to the ICE and IC/EC networks of Deutsche Bahn and has local con-nections (S-Bahn trains) run by the regional trans-port authority Verkehrsver-bund Rhein-Neckar
www.vrn.de

BY AIR: City Airport Man-nheim, approx. 15 km away, is connected with Heidel-berg via tram line no. 5
www.flugplatz-mannheim.de

Frankfurt Airport is ap-prox. 80 km away (*www.frankfurt-airport.de*). Connections from there to hotels via the TLS Shuttle Service Frankfurt:
tel. 06221/770077
www.tls-heidelberg.de
Baden-Airpark, the air-port for Karlsruhe/Baden-Baden, is approx. 90 km from Heidelberg (*www.baden-airpark.de*) and is reached via the Baden-Airpark-Express Shuttlebus from Heidel-berg railway station.
The distance to **Stuttgart Airport** (*www.flughafen-stuttgart.de*), about 120 km, can be covered in some 50 minutes by the S-Bahn train service.
From **Frankfurt Hahn Airport** (approx. 150 km from Heidelberg) the Hahn Express Shuttlebus goes to the railway station:
www.holger-tours.de

● **HEIDELBERG MAIN STATION**
Willy-Brandt-Platz 5
69115 Heidelberg
tel.: 030/2970
www.bahnhof.de
◆ DDB Reisezentrum (travel centre) in the main station: Buses and trams stop in front of the main railway station.
Taxis wait at the first exit (east exit) on the right (between the tobacconist and the newsagent).

CAR HIRE: Europcar,
DB Reisezentrum,

BICYCLES: Call a Bike in
front of the station (*www.
callabike.de*),
Heidel-bike
Rohrbacher Straße 13-15
www.heidel-bike.de

BANKS

● **REISEBANK**
Heidelberg main rail
station

HEIDELBERGCARD

The HeidelbergCARD is valid
according to preference
for 1, 2 or 4 days, or as a
family ticket for two days.
It gives you free rides on
public transport, admission
to the castle including
the trip there and back
by funicular railway, and
reduced prices for guided
walks, tours, museums and
exhibitions, admission to
cultural and leisure facilities, restaurants and shops.
The HeidelbergCARD can
be purchased in the tourist
information centres at the
main railway station and in
the city hall, at Touristser-
vice Neckarmünzplatz, in

the Kurpfälzisches Museum
and in many of Heidel-
berg's hotels.

BOX OFFICE

● **KULTURHAUS
KARLSTORBAHNHOF**
Am Karlstor 1
www.karlstorbahnhof.de

● **THEATERKASSE**
Theaterstraße 10
www.theaterheidelberg.de

MEDIA

PRINT: Rhein-Neckar-
Zeitung, Wochenkurier
TV AND RADIO: Süd-
westrundfunk, Campus-
radio Rhein-Neckar, Rhein-
Neckar Fernsehen

EMERGENCY

Police: tel. 110
Fire brigade: tel. 112
Ambulance: tel. 19 222
(from mobile phone dial
06221 first)
Emergency doctor:
tel. 06221/19292
**Private emergency
doctor:** tel. 01805/304505
Emergency dentist:
tel. 06221/3544917
Emergency pharmacy:
tel. 01805/002963

ADAC breakdown service:
tel. 089/20204000
Lost and found:
tel. 06221/653797
Help line:
tel. 0800/1110111

PUBLIC TRANSPORT

● **RHEIN-NECKAR-
VERKEHR GMBH (RNV)**
Sales office in main
station
Kurfürstenanlage 62
Service number:
www.rnv-online.de

Up-to-date information is
available via the *rnv Start.
Info-App* for iPhone and
Android.

CITY TOURS

Heidelberg Marketing:
www.heidelberg-marketing.de

TAXI

● **TAXIZENTRALE**
tel. 06221/302030

● **TAXI DIREKT**
tel. 06221/739090

● **CORNELIUS SCHIECK
LIMOUSINENSERVICE**
tel. 06221/164664

Heidelberg's History

Around 450 BC	Celts settle on the Heiligenberg.
80 AD	The Romans build a bridge across the Rhine.
1196	First written mention of Heidelberg.
1303	First evidence of a castle.
1386	Prince Elector Ruprecht I founds the university, the third in the Holy Roman Empire after those in Prague and Vienna.
1392	Prince Elector Ruprecht II extends the town to the west.
1400-1410	Prince Elector Ruprecht III, in his capacity as Ruprecht I, King of the Germans, founds the Church of the Holy Spirit as a burial church for the electors.
1518	Martin Luther's Heidelberg Disputation.
1556	Prince Elector Ottheinrich introduces the Reformation to the Electoral Palatinate.
1563	Publication of the Heidelberg Catechism makes the town a bastion of Calvinism.
1613	Prince Elector Friedrich V marries Elizabeth Stuart, daughter of James I of England.
1622	After the capture of Heidelberg by the forces of the Catholic League under General Tilly, the Bibliotheca Palatina is taken to the Vatican.
1689 und 1693	The town and castle are destroyed by French troops during the War of the Palatinate Succession.
1703	Completion of the town hall.
1720	Prince Elector Carl Philipp moves his residence to Mannheim, the new capital of the Palatinate.

1788 A stone bridge, the Alte Brücke, is built by Prince Elector Carl Theodor.

1803 Heidelberg is incorporated in Baden. In the reign of Karl-Friedrich the university is renamed Ruperto Carola.

1871 Friedrich Ebert, later the first president of the German Reich, is born in Heidelberg.

1903 The physician Vinzenz Czerny founds an institute for experimental research into cancer, the forerunner of the German Cancer Research Center.

1907 The lower jaw of "Homo heidelbergensis" is discovered in Mauer.

1930 Foundation of the New University.

1945 Heidelberg, largely undamaged by the war, is occupied by American military forces and is later the headquarters of the US Army and NATO.

1964 Foundation of the German Cancer Research Center.

1967 The Max Planck Institute for Astronomy (MPIA) is founded on the Königstuhl.

2000 Opening of the Print-Media-Akademie of Heidelberger Druckmaschinen AG.

2007 Heidelberg University is officially awarded the title of elite university by the German federal government.

2012 The first residents move into the new district of Bahnstadt.

2013 The US Army has vacated all of its bases in Heidelberg.

2014 Stefan W. Hell, a professor at the University of Heidelberg, receives the Nobel Prize in Chemistry.

2019 the first company moves to the Heidelberg Innovation Park, the ideas quarter for the digital world.

Picture Credits:
All photos BKB Verlag except Adobe Stock/eyetronic U1; BHP Agentur für Bild und Konzept GmbH 50 be., Chocolaterie St. Anna No 1 39 be., 70 ab.l., DKFZ/Tobias Schwerdt 21 Mi., EMBL 68, Galerie Edition Staeck 63 Mi., Heidelberger Zuckerladen 49, Heidelberg Marketing GmbH 16 be., 32 be., 37, 55 be., 62 ab., Mi.; Heidelberg Marketing GmbH/Christoph Duepper 17; Heidelberg Marketing GmbH/Haeuser 40 Mi.; Heidelberg Marketing GmbH/Rothe 54 ab.; Heidelberg Marketing Gmbh/Tobias Schwerdt 25 ab., 56-57 ab.; Heidelberg Suites Boutique Hotel 50 ab., Internationales Musikfestival Heidelberger Frühling gGmbH/Sven Hoppe 60 l., Institut für Geowissenschaften 64 ab., iStock/jimfeng U6; Jazzhaus Heidelberg 25 be., 61 be., Landesmedienzentrum Ba.-Wü. U1 ab., 44 ab.l., 71 ab.l., Leanders Leseladen 66 Mi., Staatliche Schlösser und Gärten Ba.-Wü. 27, Stiftung Reichspräsident-Friedrich-Ebert-Gedenkstätte.de 15 ab., Mi.; Textilsammlung Max Berk, Kurpfälzisches Museum 65 ab., Theater und Orchester Heidelberg/ Florian Merdes 60-61 ab., Theater und Orchester Heidelberg/Kalle Kuikkaniemi 62-63 be., Universität Heidelberg – Kommunikation und Marketing 17, 18 ab., 20 be., Vinyl Only 67 be., www.pixabay/Herbert Aust 14 ab.; www.pixabay.com/rohatcom68 27 ab.; Zoo Heidelberg 46 ab.

3 Days in
HEIDELBERG

Make the
most of
your time!

HEIDELBERG
AT A GLANCE

3 Days in

University · City Walk · Heidelberg by Night · Kurpfälzisches Museum · The Castle · Schwetzingen Palace · Philosophers' Path · Strolling and Shopping